The Anger Worl
Book for Teens

Jan Stewart

Jalmar Press

The Anger Workout Book for Teens

Copyright © 2002 by Jan Stewart

Jalmar Press
Permission's Department
P.O. Box 1185
Torrance, Calfornia 90505

(310)816-3085
fax: (310)816-3092
e-mail: jalmar@worldnet.att.net
www.jalmarpress.com

Published by Jalmar Press
ISBN: 1-931061-13-0

Cover design: Linda Jean Thille
Interior design: Jeanne Iler
Illustrations: Michael V. Prochazka, Jeanne Iler,
and North Light Clip Art

Manufacturered in the United States of America
10 9 8 7 6 5 4 3 2

Dedication

Be angry, but do something
admirable with it.
Anger is not an excuse to hurt.

For Jack

CONTENTS

CONTENTS

Anger Workouts

INTRODUCTION

What Is It?

The Anger Workout Book for Teens is a collection of thirty-eight workouts (lessons) for secondary students. Each workout comes with coach notes to help the teacher or counselors organize the lesson as well as reproducible student activity sheets. The student activities and implementation strategies were carefully written to address multiple learning styles: drama, games, abstract art, interpersonal and intrapersonal activities, logical reasoning and problem solving, music and movement. By using these multiple learning styles, students learn anger-management skills that they can understand and use. Every workout follows similar format and includes learning objectives, discussion questions, processing activities, and follow-up learning projects. *The Anger Workout Book for Teens* was developed to help students learn about anger and learn specific tips and techniques to help them manage their own anger more effectively. The entire book relies on sport analogies and sports-related terms so that the material is more relevant and interesting to teens. Secondary students often have an interest in sports either watching or taking part themselves. It seemed like a great way to have fun and motivate students into learning.

Why Anger?

It doesn't matter where you are from, anger will affect you in some way or another. From road rage to school shootings, anger is around us. Whether we experience it directly or merely hear about it in the news, anger is a serious problem. When anger is not dealt with properly, it leaves its mark on us both physically and emotionally. As educators we are often the only ones that have a chance to change the perceptions about anger and teach our youth more effective ways to manage anger. We cannot expect all of our students to know how to handle anger. Like any other skill, it must be taught and practiced, reinforced and reviewed.

Why should it be taught at school? Why not? Kids are not going to learn the skills when they are immersed in a violent and abusive environment or when they are inundated by movies, videos and television shows that promote fighting and other forms of violence. The school is often the only place that does not tolerate violence and in some cases it is the only safe and accepting environment for a student.

Ask any teacher, counselor, school administrator, or parent what they think teens need help with, and you will hear the word "anger" come up fairly often. Pretty much everyone could use a little brushing up on their anger-management skills. Dealing more effectively with your own anger or learning to cope with other people's anger is a life long skill that we could all use some help with. Working as a high school counselor, I have had the opportunity to work with many students over the years with issues of depression, suicidal thoughts, frustration, self-destructive behaviors, and academic difficulties. Talking to students for an extended period of time, will almost always uncover related anger issues. Anger is the root of many other presenting issues and when it is not properly managed, it certainly leads to many other problems later in life.

Why A Book?

As a high school counselor, I am often asked to come into classrooms to talk about anger-management. By far, anger-management has been at the top of the most wanted list by teachers I have worked with at each school level, elementary, middle, and high school. A lot of different skills fall under the anger-management umbrella: mediation, self-expression, assertiveness training, relaxation and stress reduction, self-talk, self-care, wellness, goal-setting and mediation. These are only some of the related topics of anger-management. As a counselor, I really needed to have one resource that tied it all together and was actually fun and easy to teach. I like having books that I can pick up and use immediately with out a lot of preparation. Let's face it, some days I just can't come up with the exact words or discussion questions to get the concept across. I know what I want to say, but getting it across to 25 at-risk and hard to teach adolescents is no simple task. I need the information organized and in front of me so that I can focus on interacting with my students. I started saving all of my workable lessons. These are the ones that I got a good response from or the ones that I got really excited about when teaching. In no time at all, I had a pretty good collection of lessons that worked. I spent a summer making sense out of them and putting them into a format that other counselors and teachers could understand.

Who Is It For?

The anger workouts were developed for classroom and small group use, however, the student activity sheets can be easily adapted for individual use.

How Are The Workouts Organized?

Each workout comes with one or two pages of "Coach Notes". This is the teacher/counselor reference page. The teacher may want to follow it exactly or use it as a general guide or reference page. Each group will be different and the teacher will be the best person to determine the format for the lesson. Most of the workouts are designed for one class period (50-60 minutes). Depending on the level and interest of the students, the time for a workout will vary.

The Coach Notes Are Divided Into 6 Stages

 ## 1. Orientation

This section includes background notes and supporting information. The notes are written to the student. This section is best used as a general introduction to the workout. The teacher may want to read it aloud to the class or copy the information onto a paper or overhead so that each student is able to read it. A lot of the Orientation is knowledge-based, and it is expected that the students understand the concepts before proceeding with the rest of the lesson. The Orientation Section might also be given to the students in note form. Many of the review questions will be taken from these sections.

 ## 2. The Challenge

This section outlines the specific learning outcomes or objectives for the workout. It is expected that the students will achieve the learning outcomes for each workout.

 ## 3. Warm-Up

This section includes group discussion questions. Some of the questions can simply be answered with a "yes" or "no", while others require a more developed response. Using a combination of open-ended, divergent, and convergent questions, the teacher is able to identify what the students know and what the students need to learn. In some cases, the students are asked to physically move to a certain area of the room to represent their answer. This section is designed to get the students thinking about a concept and introduce them to new terms and ideas.

 ## 4. Workout

The workout is the main part of the lesson. Each workout includes the student activity sheet as well as additional work done as a class, in a small group or individually.

 ## 5. Cool Down

This section was developed to further process the work done in the workout. It usually brings the class together again and acts as a debriefing session or else a time where the students can discuss work they have done individually.

 ## 6. Breakaway

This section offers additional activities related to the general theme of the workout. Numerous suggestions are included using a variety of techniques such as art, drama, interviews, surveys, looking at different sources of media, and numerous other language related activities. The teacher may want to use all of the activities or only a few. Each Break-Away Activity can also be easily modified or expanded.

How Do I Best Use This Book?

The workouts would be excellent to use in an anger-management group or as a curriculum for classroom guidance. Although the workouts are logically organized, they can be completed randomly. Something to keep in mind is that Workouts 1-18 are reviewed in Workout 18 — The Angry 8's Half-Time Game, and Workouts 19-38 are reviewed in Workout 37 — The Endurance Run With Hurdles. Workout 38 — The Super Bowl is a review of all 38 workouts. Start with giving each student a copy of "Introductory Information for Students" found on the next page.

If some of the workouts are omitted, it would be helpful to give the students the basic information from the orientation section of the omitted workouts so they can still play the review games.

Why A Journal?

Most of the workouts include a self-reflection activity where the student is asked to write their personal thoughts in a private journal. In some cases they are asked to reflect on a particular activity, consider another situation, answer specific questions, or respond to something discussed in the class. This process is a valuable tool for the student to keep track of their own growth and development throughout the workouts. Whether they work through all 38 workouts or only just a few, a personal journal will be an excellent learning tool and self-monitoring exercise. It is suggested that students get a bound book (as opposed to three-hole punched sheets) so that all of the pages stay together. When students do not feel like writing, a great substitute would be to draw. It is important to save all work, even scribbles, doodles and notes. Everything stays.

What Now?

Flip through the workouts and get a feel for the format. Pick a workout, read through the coach notes, gather whatever you need for the workout, and give it a try.

Author Note

While I support the need to be all-inclusive, I find the use of "he/she," "s/he," and "he or she" cumbersome in writing. For the sake of simplicity, I alternate between the masculine and feminine pronouns wherever appropriate.

Introductory Information for Students

This workout book is not an intense therapy or treatment program. It is a training program and a total fitness program for the whole body including mental, social, physical, and emotional. *The Anger Workout Book for Teens* is a series of activities to help you deal more effectively with anger. No one is perfect, and we don't expect you to do everything right all of the time. What is important, however, is improving yourself and keeping your mind open to being a better person. Training yourself to become aware of your thoughts and feelings, your attitudes and behaviors will help you control anger. Just like any training program, anger-management training works best if it is done over a long period of time. Making smaller steps towards a goal is better than taking no steps at all. Be patient with yourself and others and you will see tremendous rewards.

Just like an athlete, if you do not maintain your program, you will regress. Your muscles might atrophy and your endurance level decrease. If you don't apply what you have learned, then it will be forgotten. Keep practicing, reviewing, and applying what you learn. Being able to transfer what you learn to your real life is the single most important aspect of any training program. If you don't use it, you will lose it!

Scaling The Anger Wall
Coach Notes

 1. Orientation

Everyone has a different tolerance level. What really angers some people may only slightly annoy others. Each of us also use different words to label the various degrees of anger. Our "anger scale" will also vary depending on our life experiences. For some people yelling and screaming is a common daily event, whereas for others, it rarely ever occurs. In the first case, the person would say yelling would be a low level, for example a 2 out of 10. The second person would likely rate screaming as a 7 or 8. If you are able to define and rate different levels of anger and indicate what would make you feel this way, you will be on your way to gaining more knowledge and control over anger.

 2. The Challenge

- Classify 10 different kinds/levels of anger.
- Rate the 10 different kinds from mildest to most severe.
- Identify incidents that could occur in their life that would make them reach the different levels of anger.

 3. Warm-Up

- Display three charts around the room and label them "mild," "moderate," and "severe."
- Read through a variety of scenarios and have the students get up and move to the level of anger chart that they feel the scenario would justify.
- <u>Scenarios might include:</u>
  You discovered your girlfriend or boyfriend cheated on you.
  Your car broke down, and it will cost $1000 to fix.
  A friend lies to you.
  You play your worst game ever, and you lose the tournament.
  At a party someone steals money from you.
  Your best friend ignores you.
  Someone insults you.
  A parent yells at you for no known reason.

 4. Work Out

- Brainstorm a list of words to represent different levels or degrees of anger.
- Have students complete the activity sheet using their own words, or the words given in class and on the sheet.

5. Cool Down

- Ask volunteers to share their answers with the class. This will allow the students to observe the variety of answers and differences of opinion regarding different degrees of anger. Discuss the differences.
- Record only three anger levels: **1-mild**, **5-moderate**, and **10-severe** on separate poster boards. On another piece of poster board, list the corresponding behavior that would result in the student feeling that anger.

 ## 6. Breakaway

- Give each student a large sheet of white paper. Distribute a variety of colored paints and brushes or another color medium, e.g., felt markers, colored pencils, crayons. Paint works best because it can run and splatter. Have each student develop a picture to express anger without using words. Display and discuss the visual interpretations.
- Develop one of the anger words into a piece of work. For example, a student could use the word "agitated" and make all of the letters "jittery". Show the feeling through the visual representation of the word. For a variation, have students act out the word.
- Read through a variety of anger situations (teacher or student generated) and ask each student to give it a rating from 1-10. Write the number on the card and then hold it up like a diving or figure-skating judge.

Scaling The Anger Wall

Activity Sheet

The scale below shows different degrees of anger. On the left side of the scale, list different kinds of anger ranging from the mildest form (1) to the most severe form (10). On the other side of the scale, list possible events that would lead to you feeling this kind of anger.

For example: If you label #1 as being slightly agitated, you may indicate that someone who stares at you would make you feel this way.

Some common words that people use to describe different levels of anger are: miffed, ticked off, enraged, annoyed, agitated, irritated, fury, incensed, infuriated, aggressive, bothered, troubled, exasperated, antagonized, crazed, frantic, mad, and violent. You may want to use the words: **mild, moderate, or severe** to further describe the level of anger.

Fill in the following chart to the best of your ability.

Kind of Anger	Level	What would cause you to feel this way?
_____	10	_____
_____	9	_____
_____	8	_____
_____	7	_____
_____	6	_____
_____	5	_____
_____	4	_____
_____	3	_____
_____	2	_____
_____	1	_____

What's Blowing Your Sails?

Workout **2**

Coach Notes

 1. Orientation

Many different situations can occur that may lead to you getting angry. Everyone will have their own tolerance level and people will respond differently to a particular situation. Each individual will see every situation from their own perspective. How you view an event will have a lot to do with how you respond. Just because you perceive certain things to be a particular way, doesn't mean that is exactly how others will perceive it.

Anger is closely related to other emotions. Often we respond as if we were angry, yet what we feel on the inside is a completely different emotion. Anger tends to be the mask of several other feelings such as hurt, fear, frustration, shame, guilt, sadness, jealousy, annoyance, disappointment, and loneliness. Although these feelings are often at the root of anger, we may also be totally unsure about how we are feeling and anger may be the only thing we recognize.

 2. The Challenge
- Learn the four main reasons for people feeling angry.
- Examine a variety of situations to determine the underlying feelings behind the anger.
- Practice looking at an issue from the perspective of another person.

 3. Warm-Up
- Why do we get angry?
- Why is anger such a common feeling?
- What other feelings accompany anger?
- What feelings are difficult to express?
- Why is it difficult to express these other feelings?

 4. Workout
- Distribute the activity sheets and have the students decide what is behind the outward expression of anger. Put the number of the scenario into the pie diagram.
- Ask each student to write three of their own scenarios and add the appropriate number to the pie.
- Go back to the ten scenarios and write down how the other person would perceive the situation. For example, what would the friend think of Juanita in the first scenario. Look at the situation from the perspective of the person who was the target of the anger.

5. Cool Down

- Discuss each scenario and determine where it best fits on the pie diagram.
- Ask volunteers to read their original scenarios. Ask other students to guess where they fit in the situation.

 ## 6. Breakaway

- Go through several newspapers and find articles that relate to anger. Cut and paste the articles on a poster. Below each article, list the reason for the anger as well as some of the other feelings that the people might also have.
- Ask the students to make a "For" and "Against" list relating to a debatable topic such as: capital punishment, smoking in public places, testing on animals. Have them work with a partner and write one side each and then switch and add to each other's list. Explain that the purpose is to see some thing from two different sides. Encourage the students to formally debate the issue in front of the class.
- For homework, have each student keep a "feeling" sheet while they watch a movie. Write the name of the movie on the top. Separate the sheet into 15 minute intervals and record all of the different feelings they encounter as they watch the movie. Bring it to a subsequent class to discuss. Collate all of the feelings on a master list to reference in later workouts.

What's Blowing Your Sails?

Activity Sheet

Typically, there are four main reasons that cause most people to feel angry:

1. **Injustice:** when we perceive that something is not fair or we are treated unfairly.
2. **Frustration**: when we are not able to perform or carry out a task that, we think, we should.
3. **Being Insulted**: when we feel that we are being attacked, insulted, or put down.
4. **Loss of Control**: when we feel that we lack control over ourselves or a particular situation.

In many cases, how we feel on the inside is quite different from what we show others on the outside.

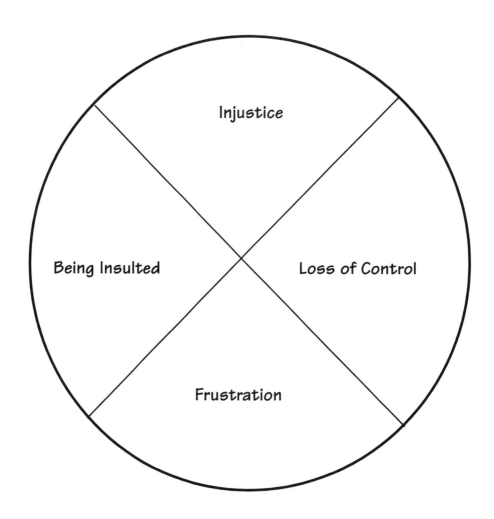

Read each scenario and determine the underlying feeling. Put the number of the scenario into the section of the pie where it best fits.

1. Juanita's friend was diagnosed with cancer. Ever since she found out, she has been yelling at people, swearing a lot, and not smiling for over two weeks. She does not know what to say to her friend so Juanita avoids her.

2. Drew's mom insists that he call her to say where he is going. On one particular night, he called home and she took a while to answer. Drew slammed the phone down and didn't call back.

3. Liam has a difficult time with math. When the teacher took too long to help him, he threw his book down and stormed out of the class.

4. Sujit's friend made a comment about his ripped shirt. He turned around and slugged him in the arm.

5. Emily turned in an assignment two days late. The teacher refused to pass her. She told off the teacher then walked out.

6. Pete usually makes over ten baskets a game. This one game he did not get a basket. Pete walks off the court, throws his towel down, slams his locker shut, and leaves.

7. Almost everyone on the team played for half the game. Urmie only played five minutes. Without talking to the coach, she sits on the bench, scowls at her teammates, and refuses to talk to any one.

8. Elandro's friend told him he was way too short to be on the team. Elandro swears at his friend and walks away.

9. Hanna's boyfriend is moving out of state. Since she found out, she hasn't said a word to him.

10. With only two weeks left of school, Amber finds out she won't graduate. She storms into the school office, yells at the office workers, and demands to speak to the principal.

Your turn. Write three situations of your own and add the number to the pie.

11. _____

_____

12. _____

_____

13. _____

_____

Obstacle Course

Workout **3**

Coach Notes

 1. Orientation

Anger can be helpful or harmful. Anger can make you stand up for yourself or anger can lead to you or to someone else getting hurt. You can use anger to help you be courageous and overcome obstacles or achieve a certain goal. Anger can help you solve a problem or make a change. Anger acts as a warning to you that something is wrong. Being angry can also lead to inappropriate expressions that can hurt you as well as others. The more intense and frequent you get angry, the more harmful it may be in the long term. How you express anger and who it affects will also determine how harmful it is. However, there are specific tips to help you deal more positively with your anger. Recognizing when you are angry, understanding why you get angry, learning to express your anger in acceptable ways, and dealing with anger from others will allow you to cope more effectively.

 2. The Challenge
- List ways that anger can be helpful or harmful.
- Learn how people have used their anger to overcome obstacles, make a positive impact on the world, or stand up for something they believe.

 3. Warm-Up
- When is anger harmful?
- When is anger helpful?
- Who are some people from the past that have hurt themselves or others with their anger?
- Who are some people from the past that have turned their anger into something good? Good examples are Martin Luther King and Rosa Parks.
- Brainstorm and create a list of the choices we all make:
  1. choose to work.
  2. choose your friends.
  3. choose what you say and do.
  4. choose to be kind or nasty.
  5. choose to be accepting or discriminating, etc.

4. Workout
- Using the activity sheet, identify a person who has used their anger to do something good, to overcome an obstacle, to challenge themself, or to make a difference in the world.
- Write about what they did with their anger.

5. Cool Down

- Have the students read out loud their short story and create a list of all of the people they learned about.
- Reinforce the idea that anger is inevitable. It is an individual choice how you deal with your anger.

6. Breakaway

- Make an anthology out of the short stories.
- Role-play a situation where someone uses anger to do something positive for themselves or others.
- Imagine different scenarios and write a positive way to overcome each situation.
  For example:
  1. You bought a car, and it broke down the first day.
  2. Someone unjustly accuses you of stealing.
  3. You were turned down for a job you really needed.
  4. You failed the only course you needed to graduate.
- Have the students write examples of their own situations and ways to overcome them.
- Have someone visit the class to talk about how they overcame their anger to do something good for society or for themselves. An example would be a person who lost an arm in a car accident and now helps teens understand safe driving. Use a speaker that students can easily relate to this life situation.

Obstacle Course

Activity Sheet

Lance Armstrong

At age 25, Lance Armstrong was one of the world's best cyclists. Lance's career was taking off and his future looked extremely bright. Then he was diagnosed with testicular cancer. Lance's cancer spread to his abdomen, lungs, and his brain. His chances were looking dim. He decided to declare himself a survivor. He learned about the disease, he underwent aggressive treatment, and he had insurmountable strength and determination to overcome this obstacle. Lance has now gone on to win his third consecutive Tour De France — the world's toughest cycling event.

Rosa Parks

On December 1, 1955, Rosa Parks, an African-American seamstress, was arrested in Montgomery, Alabama, for not giving up her seat on a bus to a white man. At this time in the American South, it was a rule that African-American riders had to sit at the back of the bus. They were expected to give up their seats to a white bus riders. Rosa did not argue or move when she was told. The police were called and she was arrested. This started the Montgomery Bus Boycott and the beginning of the Civil Rights Movement which led to local, state, and federal civil rights laws being passed.

Write a story of someone from the past or present who has overcome anger or another obstacle to make a difference in the world.

List some of the obstacles you have overcome in your life.

_____

_____

_____

_____

_____

_____

_____

Now read through your list and circle the obstacles that were accompanied with some degree of anger.

Body Talk

Coach Notes

 1. Orientation

   Have you ever just stopped what you were doing and noticed that your shoulders are way up by your ears, or your heart is pounding at an alarming speed? When you have a big argument with someone do you find yourself with a headache or a stomachache a few hours later? This is how your body talks to you. The body responds physically when it is stressed, alarmed, scared, bored, happy, sad, or worried. If you can't hear your body talk, then you won't know when to take care of it. If you choose not to take care of your body then look out the results can be disastrous.

2. The Challenge

   - Identify personal physical responses to anger.
   - List long term and short term effects of anger, tension, and stress.
   - Illustrate how an angry person would look like.

3. Warm-Up

   - How can you tell that you are getting angry?
   - How many of you turn red? Get tense? Start sweating? Feel sick or nauseous? Have a hard time thinking straight?
   - What do you typically do when you notice these signs?
   - What happens when you ignore your body signs and continue getting angrier?
   - What are some of the short-term physical effects of anger, tension, stress when it is not dealt with positively? Do you get a migraine headache or feel nausea?
   - What are some of the long-term physical effects of anger, tension, or stress when it is not dealt with positively? Do you have high blood pressure, ulcers, colitis, or back problems?

4. Workout

   - Complete the physical signs checklist on the activity sheet.
   - Sketch a picture of someone who is angry and label all of the signs and symptoms.

5. Cool Down

   - Share your picture with a partner and discuss the similarities and differences.
   - Explain that numerous, positive coping strategies for anger, tension, or stress will be discussed in later workouts.

 **6. Breakaway**

- Use magazines and cutout portions to illustrate an angry person.
- Make a montage (A pictorial composition made by closely arranging or super-imposing many pictures or designs.) out of the anger illustrations.
- Have the class work in groups of six to develop a group drawing of an angry person. Pass the same picture around to each person. Have each student add one sign or symptom of anger to the picture and pass it on. Give each person a set amount of time then pass it to someone else.
- Invite a doctor or physiotherapist to talk about treatments for people who suffer from stress-related illnesses like migraine headaches, ulcers, back problems, etc.
- Have one student act out a sign or symptom. Then have the class guess which one it is. List all the symptoms on separate slips of paper and put them into an envelope for students to pick from. This activity can also be done with teams competing against each other.

Body Talk

Workout  4

Activity Sheet

When we are angry our bodies will physically respond in a variety of ways. These are all natural reactions to something that threatens or angers us. You may notice all or only some of the following signs. Everyone will respond differently to things or to people that anger them.

Put a checkmark beside the responses that you typically experience when you are angry.

___ Increased rate of breathing or heavy breathing.
___ Dry mouth.
___ Increased heart rate.
___ Increased blood pressure.
___ Flushed face.
___ Dilated pupils.
___ Clenched hands.
___ Tense muscles.
___ Headache.
___ Stomachache.
___ Increased adrenaline flow.
___ Warm sweaty skin.
___ Numbness.
___ Difficulty thinking.
___ Shaking or trembling.

What other signs or symptoms do you experience? _____

_____

Now that you know how your body talks to you. **LISTEN.** Many people can hear their body talking but they refuse to listen. After a while, they realize that they have irreversible health problems or they find out that they need to make a dramatic change in their life in order to be healthy again. Remember you only have one body so take good care of it.

Most people have a hard time dealing with anger. If you find anger a difficult emotion to handle, you are not alone. Managing anger takes a lot of hard work, but over time you will notice definite benefits to learning these new anger-management skills. Anger-management techniques can help you at school, in a job, and with your family, friends, and other relationships.

On the other side of this Activity Sheet, sketch a picture of an angry person. Sketch simply or cartoon the person.

Preventer or Provoker

Coach Notes

1. Orientation

Taking a look at how you respond to particular situations will help you gain some insight into how your thinking influences your anger. Remember that how you perceive certain events will have a lot to do with how angry you will get. For example if you walk out of a store and someone bumps into you, you may think to yourself "What a jerk, he should watch where he is going." The other option would be "Oh well, accidents happen, so what if he didn't see me." The first example would likely lead to an anger response. The second example would likely never amount to anything and just another event that you encounter throughout your day.

Scuba Divers can teach us a lot about preventing attacks. The underwater world is completely different from land. There are unknown fish, dangerous predators, poisonous plants and deadly animals. The key to safety is to leave everyone and everything alone. Don't go around stirring things up, provoking others, or meddling with plants. If you stick to yourself, you will be left alone but if you agitate the surroundings, you will likely get hurt. Don't disturb the environment just observe the environment.

An encounter can happen to you, but it is your choice whether you get angry or not. You can shrug it off or you can attack it.

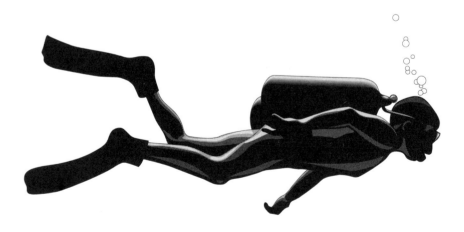

2. The Challenge
- Complete a self-assessment survey related to typical anger-inducing situations.
- Learn the difference between a provoking response and a preventative response to an incident.

 ## 3. Warm-Up
- Are there particular situations that often anger you?
- Do similar situations anger everyone?
- Are there times that you get really angry at a particular situation and then other times the same situation would hardly even bother you?
- What makes people more susceptible to anger?
- What makes people more understanding and forgiving?

 ## 4. Workout
- Complete the Preventer or Provoker Self-assessment.
- Using the grading scale on the last page, score the responses. It is easier for the teacher to read through the scale and have the students look at their answers so they do not have to flip back and forth.

5. Cool Down
- Have students write responses to the survey in a journal.
- Discuss what kinds of situations or scenarios seem to be the most anger-inducing.
- Were there some questions that you would have reacted totally different from the two responses provided? Write what response you would have chosen beside the question.
- What is the key ingredient to preventing anger? Brainstorm for answers and record them on the board.

6. Breakaway
- Write ten more situations similar to the ones on the survey and provide a preventative and provoking type of response.
- Pick seven to ten questions from the survey and write a preventative response of your own.
- Write a short paragraph when you prevented anger from occurring and another paragraph when you provoked anger.
- Have a parent or friend complete the survey.
- Have groups role-play a preventative response and a provoking response.

Preventer or Provoker

Workout **5**

Activity Sheet

Read the following scenarios and circle the response that would represent how you would react. When you finish, score your responses to see where you fall on the anger response scale.

1. A hairdresser cuts off 4 inches of your hair after you told them you only wanted a trim.
    A. You tell them they did an awful job and refuse to pay.
    B. You feel bad. Next time you will ask them to show you first how much is being trimmed.

2. You are stuck in a traffic jam and have an exam that starts in 10 minutes.
    A. You get agitated, swear, and honk your horn at all the stupid drivers ahead.
    B. You are agitated but traffic jams are inevitable and there is nothing you can do about them.

3. Someone treats you unfairly.
    A. You go over and tell them off.
    B. You tell them that they are not being fair and offer a better solution.

4. Someone makes a sarcastic remark to you.
    A. They have the problem and you don't even bother yourself with their rudeness.
    B. You call them an equally sarcastic remark and threaten to hurt them if they don't shut up.

5. You are studying in a library and someone makes irritating noises at a table near you.
    A. You move to a different table and continue with your work.
    B. You sigh a few times and let them know you hear them. You tell them to get lost, if they keep it up.

6. You are in a slow moving drive-thru, and you are starving.
    A. Line-ups are unavoidable and inconvenient, but eventually you will get your food.
    B. You get ticked off and think that it must be the incompetent staff.

7. Your boyfriend or girlfriend cancels a date at the last minute.
    A. You yell at them for being inconsiderate and leaving you with nothing to do.
    B. You don't worry about it and instead go out with a friend.

8. You are trying to assemble something and just can't understand the directions.
    A. You are frustrated and throw the pieces across the room.
    B. You walk away and come back to it later.

9. A teacher criticizes your work after you spent the whole weekend revising it.
    A. You are mad and think the teacher is stupid.
    B. You see if the comments are valid and if your work needs further changes.

10. At a party, a very annoying person keeps trying to talk to you.
    A. You move away at a convenient and less obvious time.
    B. You are rude to them and hope they get the message.

11. A friend borrows something from you and informs you they lost it.
    A. You don't worry because they will likely replace it.
    B. You feel angry about their carelessness and their respect for your belongings.

12. A referee doesn't make a penalty call you think was an obvious foul.
    A. You yell at the referee because they are not paying attention, and they are obviously siding with the other team.
    B. You realize it is difficult to see everything in a game.

13. Someone in your group of friends always hogs the conversation.
    A. You wait for the best time to put them in their place.
    B. You choose to spend the least amount of time with them.

14. While playing a sport, you suspect someone has cheated.
    A. You stop playing and demand that the person confess.
    B. You continue playing after all its only a game. It's their problem if they need to cheat.

Scoring Your Responses

1. A=1, B=0	5. A=0, B=1	9. A=1, B=0	13. A=0, B=1
2. A=1, B=0	6. A=1, B=0	10. A=0, B=1	14. A=0, B=1
3. A=1, B=0	7. A=1, B=0	11. A=1, B=0	
4. A=0, B=1	8. A=0, B=1	12. A=1, B=0	

If you scored over 12 points: Your actions likely provoke others and make them angrier. You probably get angry very quickly and you often find the behavior of others unacceptable. You would greatly benefit from learning some strategies to reduce and prevent anger.

If you scored between 8-12 points: You likely experience a moderate amount of anger on a fairly regular basis. Learning some new strategies and changing some of your thinking styles would help you out. There are many ways you can improve to help prevent anger.

If you scored between 4-7 points: Some of your actions and thoughts could be improved in order to reduce the anger in your life.

If you score below 4 points: You have developed some very useful strategies for controlling anger. Your thinking and behavior allows you to prevent many angry situations from developing. There are still areas that could be improved, but you are doing quite well. Give yourself a pat on the back for your patience.

Reaction Time

Coach Notes

 1. Orientation

There are three ways that people generally express their anger: aggressive, passive, and assertive.

Aggressive people demand their rights without thinking about the rights of others. This type of anger hurts people either emotionally, physically, or psychologically. Passive people keep their anger inside and do not like to deal with the issue. They are often quiet and do not get what they really want. Assertive people stand up for their rights and at the same time they respect the rights of others. Anger is expressed directly and in a non-threatening manner. Assertive people use a variety of techniques to respond to anger.

 2. The Challenge

- Examine personal thoughts about anger.
- Complete an assessment on personal style of expressing anger.
- Learn the difference between passive, assertive, and aggressive behavior.

 3. Warm-Up

- What words come to mind when you hear the word "anger?" What do people think about anger? How do people learn to express their anger?
- How were emotions expressed in your family? How did people in your family handle anger and solve conflicts? How has your up-bringing affected your anger?

 4. Workout

- Complete the anger questionnaire individually.
- Discuss the three terms: aggressive, assertive, and passive.
- Write the three terms on separate cards and hang them in three different places around the room.
- Read through the anger questionnaire again and have the students classify the responses as assertive, aggressive, or passive. Have the students physically stand near the cards on display.
- For larger groups, give each student an index card to write the three words: assertive, aggressive, or passive. Then ask the students to hold up their appropriate index card as you read through the anger questionnaire.

 5. Cool Down

- Have each student list typical behaviors that match the three responses on the back of their cards or on a poster under the displayed card.
- Develop a definition for each of the three terms and write it on the cards.
- Point out that assertive people have the best results and discuss why.

- Ask each student to review the questionnaire again and write down three statements that are the most problematic for them. Then set three goals they would like to strive for over the next three to six months.
- Develop a ladder of priority. Ask each student to list seven to ten problems related to their questionnaire that they would like to work on for the next few months. Design a ladder and tell each student to start with the easiest problem (the bottom) then work their way up to the hardest problem. Ask each student to draw their Ladder of Success in their journal or on a separate sheet.

6. Breakaway

- Determine what animal best represents the three terms: aggressive, passive, and assertive. Draw or cut out a picture; paste it on a blank sheet; and, share it with the class.
- Draw an abstract picture to represent each of the three terms.
- Brainstorm sports that are passive, aggressive, or assertive and then list them.
- Brainstorm business marketing plans or selling techniques that are passive, aggressive, or assertive. Score them on a scale of 1-10 with "1" being passive, "5" being assertive, and "10" being aggressive. Explore a variety of media: magazines, newspapers, television ads, e-mail ads, internet banner ads, telemarketing, direct mail, contests, billboards. Find examples to fit the behavior styles.
- Ask students to find music that represents the three different kinds of expression.

Reaction Time

Activity Sheet

ANGER QUESTIONNAIRE

Put a check mark next to the statements that are true for you. Then go through the list again and put the letter "P" next to three statements that cause you the biggest problems.

_____ I get really angry when people disagree with me.

_____ I do not like to get angry.

_____ I would rather pretend to agree than get into an argument.

_____ I am usually the one to give in during an argument.

_____ I have been known to threaten people.

_____ If I get angry, I feel guilty later.

_____ I would rather keep my anger inside and avoid any trouble.

_____ I always think of better things to say after an argument.

_____ Things seem to make me angry very quickly.

_____ I get nervous when other people are angry.

_____ I seem to go blank when I am angry, and I can't think clearly.

_____ I just get so angry that I have to hit something.

_____ I hold grudges against people who make me mad.

_____ I ignore people who I am angry with.

_____ If someone is rude to me, I take out revenge later.

_____ I stay angry for a long time.

_____ I can go from being totally calm to completely enraged in minutes.

_____ I usually feel bad after I get angry.

_____ I usually regret my actions when I am angry.

_____ I throw things when I am really angry.

_____ Being angry is not good.

_____ Nice people don't get angry.

_____ I have a hard time forgiving people.

_____ I get so mad that sometimes I don't know what I am doing.

_____ I seem to get angry at even the littlest thing.

_____ After I explode, I feel a lot better.

_____ I tend to lose control when I am angry.

_____ I do not like to admit that I am wrong.

_____ I usually avoid people who I am angry with.

_____ I enjoy getting angry.

You can't choose the environment that you grew up in. As a child you are not responsible for how you were treated. As adults we are responsible for our thoughts, feelings, and behavior. If we did not learn positive, anger-coping skills early in life, we need to learn them now.

ESCAPE, EXPRESS, OR EXPLODE?

When you are angry, you have a choice about how you will respond.

ANGER

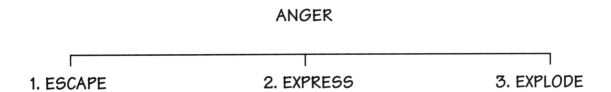

1. ESCAPE   2. EXPRESS   3. EXPLODE

1. You can escape by burying your feelings or by ignoring or avoiding the situation.
2. You can express yourself assertively by problem-solving, negotiating, or compromising.
3. You can explode by venting, blowing up, or becoming physically aggressive.

How do you picture the three responses? If you had to pick an object, animal, or plant to show the three responses, what would it be? Draw three symbols or pictures in the boxes below.

1. ESCAPE	2. EXPRESS	3. EXPLODE

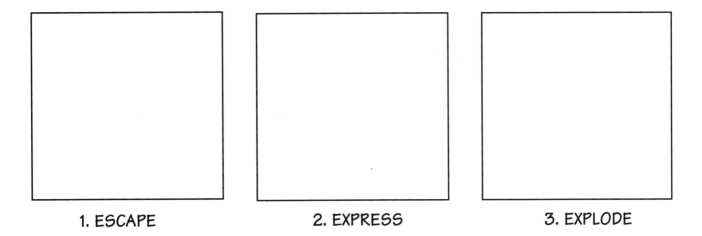

Running Track

Coach Notes

 1. Orientation

Keeping track of your anger provides the opportunity to learn more about your thoughts, feelings and behaviors. It also helps you determine the cause of your anger. After a while, you may notice some common themes or situations that seem to occur repeatedly. Gathering this information is useful because it helps you find more effective ways to deal with problem situations.

2. The Challenge

- Learn how to keep track of personal anger.
- Learn how to recognize when you are angry.
- Determine the cause of your anger.
- Find out how to take action towards solving the problem.

3. Warm-Up

- What are additional feelings you have when you are angry?
- Why would it be helpful to keep track of your anger?
- What are the important factors to track?
- What would be an example of an anger-reducing strategy?
- What is the difference between thoughts and feelings?
- What is an example of action?

4. Workout

- Discuss the three terms: recognition, causation and action.
- Have each student copy the information on the activity sheet into a daily tracking book.
- Keep a log for the duration of the workouts.
- Ask a volunteer to make-up an anger-inducing episode in order to demonstrate how to use the tracking form.

 5. Cool Down

- After a week, write a brief summary of observations and conclusions.
- Have students chart their grades each week to see their progress. Use graph paper with grades A, B, C, D or E on the vertical scale and weeks 1, 2, 3, etc. along the horizontal scale.

6. Breakaway

- Keep a daily journal of important events, interactions with people, and personal thoughts and feelings.
- Play charades having teams guess actions, thoughts, feelings and outcomes related to anger. Write words on slips of paper and ask a student to act it out without talking.
- Divide the class into small groups and have them present a series of four to six tableaus (a still life scene) to show the progression of an angry situation. For example, a team losing a tournament, a fender bender accident, or someone failing a driver's test. Have each team present their tableau to the class. Discuss the various scenes and relate them to the anger stages: <u>recognition, causation and action</u>.

Running Track

Activity Sheet

If you want to deal more effectively with your anger, there are three steps that you can follow to help you.

1. Recognition   2. Causation   3. Action

To begin, you will need to recognize how you feel, act, and think when you are angry. The best way is to pay attention to how your body reacts to different situations. The second step is to figure out why you are angry. This may be quite difficult as you will need to objectively examine the situation and determine what has ultimately caused or lead to your anger. You might need to admit that your anger is a result of something you did. The last step is to take action and work towards finding a solution to your problem or to keep your anger to yourself.

Keeping track of when you get angry will provide you with useful information about what triggers your anger. Tracking is also a very useful recording device to help you understand your own personal style of dealing with anger.

The following information should be recorded in a journal as soon as possible after an event that angers you. Use a small notebook that you can keep in a pocket or purse. Copy the following information on each page of your journal and then keep a record of your anger responses for a month.

When? (Date and time.)
Where were you?
What happened?
Your thoughts. (List.)
Your feelings. (Describe.)
Your actions. (What you did.)
Did you try any anger-reducing strategy? (List what you tried.)
What was the outcome?
What is one thing you could have done differently that would have made things turn out better?

After one week, write a brief summary of your observations and conclusions.

_____

_____

_____

_____

_____

Instant Replay

Coach Notes

 1. Orientation

When you make a mistake, fix it, and go on. If you keep going over the situation in your head thinking "I should have said this" or "I shouldn't have done that," you will waste a lot of time worrying about something you cannot do anything about. If you keep "shouldering the blame", you will only feel worse. Accept that no one is perfect. Making mistakes is the way we learn. The important thing is learning from your mistakes. Think about what went wrong; what you could have done better; and, what will you do if it happens again. Then call it quits, throw in the towel, and move on. Pick yourself up and go. An instant replay is just that instant. It doesn't continue for hours, days, or weeks.

 2. The Challenge

- List particular antecedents to anger.
- Determine what went wrong in a variety of scenarios.
- Decide what action has a more favorable outcome.

 3. Warm-Up

- What behaviors set people off or get others angry? (Name-calling, insulting remarks, raising voices, pointing fingers, and unfairness.)
- Why is it important to replay a situation that doesn't go well?
- Why is it necessary not to replay a situation over and over?
- How many people say to themselves "If only I had… or I should have said… or I should not have done that."?
- Why is this kind of talk helpful? Why is this kind of talk harmful?
- When it comes to anger, how can we learn from our mistakes?

 4. Workout

- Read through each scenario on the activity sheet and determine what went wrong and replace it with a more helpful response.

 5. Cool Down

- Read through a variety of responses for each scenario and discuss what would have made each situation turn out more positively.

 6. Breakaway

- Instead of reading through the students' answers, have them role-play their answers in a performance for the class.
- In groups, have the students write their own scenarios showing what went wrong and how it could have worked out.
- In their journal, write a personal situation that did not turn out. Then write how it could have been settled positively.

Instant Replay

Activity Sheet

The following scenarios do not end so well. In most cases the escalated anger response was unnecessary. Read each scenario and determine what went wrong. Then replay the scenario with what you think would have made things turn out a lot better.

1. José comes home one hour late after his curfew. His mom is awake and worrying about him. She is upset because she has to be at work in five hours and hasn't slept at all. When José walks in she tensely asks, "Where have you been? I have been worrying myself sick." He responds saying, "I just forgot about the time. It's no big deal." His mom raises her voice saying, "It is big deal because I couldn't get any sleep. This is the third time this has happened this month. You are now grounded!" José yells at her saying, "You over react and are too controlling." His mom yells back and says, "That if you don't follow my rules, then you can leave." José grabs his stuff and takes off.

What went wrong in this situation?_____
_____
_____

What would make this situation turn out better? _____
_____
_____

2. Matt really likes Cara and he tells his best friend, Ron about her. Ron starts paying a lot of attention to Cara. Matt starts getting jealous. Matt sees them flirting with each other and decides that it has to stop. He goes up to them and yells at Matt calling him an inconsiderate, untrusting, girlfriend stealer. Ron and Cara start laughing to themselves and tell Matt he is a paranoid idiot. He can forget about hanging out with them ever again.

What went wrong in this situation? _____
_____
_____

What would make this situation turn out better? _____
_____
_____
_____

Third Degree

Coach Notes

 1. Orientation

Think for a minute about how you know someone is angry or on the verge of blowing up? What do they look like? What do they sound like? How do they move?

Recognizing when other people are angry may help you respond in a way to prevent the situation from getting worse. Paying attention to your own cues for anger will also help you be more aware of your body. You can then calm yourself down and respond more appropriately.

2. The Challenge

- Draw, label, and define the terms: mildly agitated, annoyed, and enraged.
- Use the five senses to describe characteristics of the three degrees of anger.
- Act out the three degrees of anger.

3. Warm-Up

- Why would it be helpful to recognize the different stages of anger in ourselves and others?
- What is a cue?
- What cues are there to let you know that someone is starting to get angry?
- What is the difference between annoyed and agitated?
- What cues are there to let you know that someone is getting annoyed?
- What cues are there to let you know that someone is enraged?
- What are the five senses? How would each be affected by anger?

4. Work Out

- Write three columns on the board and label them: mildly agitated, annoyed and enraged.
- Brainstorm words that describe each anger degree.
- List the five senses on the board. Pick one of the anger degrees and describe how each sense would be affected by the degree of anger.
- Complete the activity sheet.

5. Cool Down

- Flip through magazines to find examples of the three degrees of anger.
- Collate the samples and put them on three different posters.
- Find three musical sounds that best represent the three anger degrees, e.g., the tambourine, drums, and bells.
- Use abstract symbols to represent the three degrees.

6. Breakaway

- Watch a video of people who progress through the three degrees of anger.
- Develop a role-play to show the three degrees of anger. Ask the observers to indicate when they think the degree of anger is changing by raising their hands or holding up index cards with the the three degrees of anger written on them.
- Walk outside and have students write down symbolic examples from nature that would show the degrees of anger. Chart their answers:

Mildly agitated	Annoyed	Enraged
Birds flying around	Wind picking up	Thunder storm

Third Degree

Activity Sheet

Draw and label three different pictures depicting the following degrees of anger:
1. Mildly agitated   2. Annoyed   3. Enraged.

Include specific physiological signs as well as typical behavior that you would observe.
Use the five senses to describe the three degrees.

1. Mildly Agitated

2. Annoyed

3. Enraged

If you want to be successful, it is important to
recognize anger and stop it from progressing
to the next stage or level.

Five at Five

Trace your hand five times on blank paper. Your task is to keep track of your five senses five times during one day. On each finger and your thumb write what sense you experience. Write the date in the center of your hand. What are you touching, seeing, hearing, tasting, and smelling at each time of the day?

Taking Inventory

Coach Notes

 ### 1. Orientation

Taking an objective look at how you think, feel, and act is not an easy task. Taking inventory of your strengths and weaknesses helps you determine areas you can improve and change. A personal inventory is for yourself. It is to help you grow and develop into a better person. You are likely a great person, but there is room for improvement in everyone. Unfortunately, no one is perfect. We all have areas of our character that we could work on.

 ### 2. The Challenge

- Complete an inventory of factual information related to anger and aggression.
- Complete a self-assessment scale related to anger and aggression.

 ### 3. Warm-Up

- Who can remember the last time they were angry?
- Was it today? Sometime this week? Last month? Last year?
- Why would it be helpful to gather facts about your own anger or aggression?
- How can information help you set goals and help you change?

 ### 4. Workout

- Fill out the personal inventory.

 ### 5. Cool Down

- Discuss techniques people have tried to reduce anger. Did they work? Chart the suggestions and techniques.
- Ask students to write in their journal about realizations and observations they made while completing the inventory.
- Finish the sentence "One thing I really want to learn about anger is...." Write the sentence on an index card and then hand it to your teacher/counselor.

6. Breakaway

- Imagine that there was a younger student (age 7-9) who was getting in trouble with controlling their anger. What advice would you give them? What information would be useful to help them deal with anger? Write a paragraph of helpful advice for them.

- Search the internet and newspapers for environmental issues that anger people. Find one issue to research: water pollution, lack of power, air pollution, etc. Report your findings to the class. Discuss positive and helpful ways to channel the anger in an effort to make a difference.

- Imagine that you are a counselor reading your own anger inventory. What would you say to your client? Do you have any suggestions for them? What issues do they need to work on?

31

Taking Inventory

Activity Sheet

GATHERING FACTS

1. Describe the most recent incident when you got angry and aggressive.

When? Date: _____ Time: _____

Where were you? _____

What happened? _____
_____

List your thoughts: _____

Describe your feelings: _____

Describe your actions: (Explain what you did.)
_____

What was the outcome? _____

How common is this type of incident for you?

❏ Happens often.   ❏ Hardly ever happens.   ❏ Never happened before.

2. How frequently do you get seriously angry and aggressive?

_____ Number of times per day.
_____ Number of times per week.
_____ Number of times per month.

3. What do you often get angry about?

_____
_____

4. Has your anger ever gotten you in trouble?.

	Yes	No
Have you ever been suspended from school because of your anger?	❏	❏
Have you ever been in trouble with the law because of your anger?	❏	❏
Have you ever been banned from a club, sport, or public place because of your anger?	❏	❏

5. What techniques have you tried to help yourself deal effectively with anger? Did they work? Please explain.

_____

_____

_____

_____

6. Self-Assessment

How often would you say the following behaviors occur? Use the numbers 0-4 to score.

0 = Never   2 = Occasionally

1 = Every once in a while   3 = Frequently   4 = Continually

_____	Swearing at people	_____	Putting people down
_____	Breaking things on purpose	_____	Deliberately hurting people
_____	Throwing things	_____	Yelling at people
_____	Loosing control	_____	Getting revenge
_____	Feel like beating people up	_____	Shoving, hitting, or pushing others

Add up your score to determine how much of an issue "aggression" is for you.

0 - 10 = Mild   11 -20 = Moderate   21 - 30 = Very serious   31 - 40 = Severe

FITT Test

Coach Notes

 1. Orientation

    Taking an objective look at the anger in your life can be a valuable gauge in determining whether anger is harmful. Being aware of your anger and keeping track of your experiences is the first step to gaining more control.

 2. The Challenge

- Learn how to measure anger by using the FITT Test
- Outline the thoughts and feelings of people with high and low FITT scores.
- List a variety of supports for people who have a high FITT level.

 3. Warm-Up

- What would someone's life be like if anger was a serious problem for them? What would life be like if they were in school or had a job? What would their relationships be like?
- Why is it often difficult for people to recognize that they have an anger problem?
- Think privately of a number that represents your anger problem:
  1 is the least and **10** the most serious amount. Keep this number in mind.

 4. Work Out

- Write out the FITT acronym and discuss each of the four terms: frequency, intensity, time, and type.
- Complete the FITT Test on the student activity sheet.
- Discuss places that people could seek help with their anger

 5. Cool Down

- If your close friend had a problem dealing with anger, what would you say or how would you help him or her?
- Was it difficult to remember incidents from the previous week?
- What are some other ways to keep track of your anger?

 **6. Breakaway**

- Write the day's events of someone suffering from the serious FITT level.
- Give someone new the FITT test. Do the same for another person you know. Discuss their similarities and differences. What conclusions did you draw from the results?
- In groups, design sample workouts to help people with a serious anger level.

FITT Test

Activity Sheet

Athletes use the FITT Principles to keep themselves healthy and in good shape.
1. They exercise three to five times a week.
2. They regulate their exercise intensity by measuring their target heart rate.
3. They exercise for about 30-45 minutes each time.
4. They use a variety of exercises such as: cardiovascular, strength, endurance, and flexibility.

They use the FITT Principle to remember the steps: frequency, intensity, time, and type. Measuring anger can also use the same principle. However, the individual strives to decrease the FITT level to stay healthy.

<u>**Frequency**</u> - How often do you get angry?

<u>**Intensity**</u> - How intense is your anger?

<u>**Time**</u> - How long does your anger last?

<u>**Type**</u> - Are you aggressive, violent, passive-aggressive, or assertive?

Answer the following questions as honestly as possible.

<u>**FREQUENCY:**</u> How frequent do you get angry?

_____ 1-2 times per week.

_____ 3-6 times per week.

_____ 7-10 times per week.

_____ 2-4 times a day.

_____ 4-8 times per day.

_____ More than 8 times a day.

<u>**INTENSITY:**</u> In general, how do you rate your typical response to anger?

Please circle the appropriate number.

1	2	3	4	5	6	7	8	9	10

Very
mild
response

Moderate
intensity
response

Extreme
intensity
response

35

In general, how long do you stay angry?

_____ Only a few minutes or less	_____ 9-12 hours
_____ 5-10 minutes	_____ 1-3 days
_____ 30 minutes to an hour	_____ Longer than 3 days?
_____ 1-4 hours	
_____ 5-8 hours	

How would you best describe your typical anger response?

_____	<u>Violent</u>	Do you punch, hit, kick, break, or throw things?
_____	<u>Aggressive</u>	Do you standup for yourself without regard to how you treat the other person by yelling and swearing?
_____	<u>Passive aggressive</u>	Do you talk behind a person's back, steal, or ruin their things?
_____	<u>Assertive</u>	Do you standup for yourself and still respect the rights of others; using I messages; negotiation and compromise; or, talking it out?

Use the following formula to calculate your level of FITT-ness.

$$\underline{} \text{ X } \underline{} \text{ X } \underline{} \text{ X } \underline{} = \underline{}$$

Frequency   Intensity   Time   Type   FITT-ness

FREQUENCY:

Give yourself the number in the bracket for the answer you calculated.

1-2 times per week	(1)
3-6 times per week	(2)
7-10 times per week	(3)
2-4 times a day	(3)
4-8 times ad day	(4)
more than 8 times a day	(5)

INTENSITY:

Record the number you calculated. _____

TIME:

Only a few minutes or less	(1)	9-12 hours	(3)
5-10 minutes	(2)	1-3 days	(5)
30 minutes to an hour	(2)	longer than 3 days	(6)
1-4 hours	(3)		
5-8 hours	(3)		

TYPE:

If you checked off assertive multiply by 1, for all other responses multiply by 2.

How do you compare?

Less than 10 =   Very fit! With weekly maintenance, anger is not likely to cause major problems in your life. Whatever you are doing is working. Well done!

10 - 50 =   Keep up your workouts. There is room for improvement.

50 - 100 =   Take time to work on anger.

100 - 150 =   Work regularly on the workouts dealing with anger.

Over 150 =   Seriously, take time to deal with your anger. You are in danger of experiencing harmful effects.

The Gift of Gab

Workout **12**

Coach Notes

 ### 1. Orientation

You can use self-talk to help you cope with anger. When someone says something upsetting and you notice that you are getting angry, you need to remind yourself to calm down, relax, and control your anger. Giving yourself encouragement and being confident can help you through some very difficult situations.

 ### 2. The Challenge

- Identify positive and negative styles of self-talk.
- Learn how self-talk contributes to your level of anger.
- Learn anger blocking self-talk.

 ### 3. Warm-Up

- What thoughts do you think go through the mind of a marathon runner right before the race? How about a rock-climber standing at the bottom of a mountain getting ready to climb? How about a soccer player ready to play for the world cup?

Write all of the responses on the board. Now review the responses and guess how each of these athletes would perform. What observations or conclusions did you make?

 ### 4. Workout

- How do you think these athletes would perform if they thought to themselves the following thoughts:

  "I don't think I will even get to mile 5 of the 26 miles that I need to run to finish."

  "I'll never get to the top."

  "I can't do this!"

  "We are going to get pulverized by this other team."

  "I am probably going to get injured today."

- Brainstorm a list of self-talk phrases that would increase anger.
- What self-talk phrases would be distructive to say to yourself? What would be constructive?
- Discuss the power of self-talk. How can self-talk help control anger? If you think it, you can make it happen.
- Read through the activity sheet and complete the work section.

5. Cool Down

- Share examples of helpful anger prevention self-talk.
- Have students write examples of positive self-talk on a sticky note and display the notes in the classroom.
- Discuss possible situations where these statements might be useable.
- Ask students to write in their journal self-talk phrases they will use.
- Remind students that no one else knows what they are thinking. They should do what works for them.

 ## 6. Breakaway

- Make a cue card to remember to use positive self-talk. Write down examples of anger-prevention self-talk on a business card size paper. (The computer sheets for generating business cards work well.) Have students design a motto or logo to place on the front.

For example:

| "Use it, don't lose it." | "Think First" | "Control Check" |

Keep it handy for easy reference.

- Write a cartoon related to anger using self-talk and real-talk (talking out loud).

Activity Sheet

If you were to write down everything you said to yourself over a week, you would probably fill several books. What you say to yourself, helps you understand a situation and then take action. Unfortunately, when you are angry or agitated, you often fill your head with self-talk that makes you more upset.

Do you ever say things like:
- "They've got a lot of nerve."
- "How can she do this to me."
- "I will get even."

- "I don't care about them anyway."
- "How dare he treat me like this."

If these statements run through your head, you are likely provoking yourself into getting angrier. Instead you need to calm yourself down by saying such things as:
- "I can work this out."
- "We will be able to solve this."
- "They probably do not mean to say this."

- "I can control myself."
- "How can the two of us get through this?"

This is called **ANGER PREVENTION SELF-TALK.** Now write some positive statements that you can use the next time you start feeling angry.

_____

_____

_____

When would you use these responses?

_____

_____

_____

Always remember to put "THINKING" in between your "FEELINGS" and your "BEHAVIOR."

1. FEELING   2. THINKING   3. BEHAVIOR

If you act impulsively and react to anger, you have likely forgotten Step 2.

Pump You Up

Coach Notes

 1. Orientation

Equally as important as self-talk is support talk. Support talk is what you say to others to help, encourage, support, and build-up their confidence. Helping others is a great way to be a positive team member.

 2. The Challenge

- To understand the importance of supporting others.
- List and use examples of supportive statements.

 3. Warm-Up

- Think about a time when someone said something to you that immediately lowered your confidence or brought you down when you had been excited about something.

  What did the person say? How did this affect you?

- Remember when you were nervous or worried about trying something new.

  Was there someone there to build you up and help you gain more confidence?
  What did this person do or say to help you? How did this make you feel?

- Remember when something did not turn out and someone said something to you that made you feel a lot better.

  What did the person say? How did it help?

 4. Workout

- Discuss how team members of hockey, baseball, or football support one another. What happens when they don't support each other? What supportive statements do they make?
- Complete the activity sheet individually.

 5. Cool Down

- Write a letter to a person who said something to you that has made a positive impact on you. This letter can be private (journal) or public (given to the person). Tell this person what they said and explain why it helped you at that time of your life.
- Ask the students to share examples of other ways (actions) that people have supported them. Share other examples with the class or write them down in a personal journal.

6. Breakaway

- Design a motivational poster to remind people to support one another. Think of a slogan, e.g., "Teamwork pays off!". Have students develop a visual to catch people's attention.
- Display the posters in a prominent place: school halls, office, gym, and guidance office.
- Have the students take part in a trust walk or another activity where they would need to rely on others and work together.
- In small groups, write a fictional story about how one person changed the world. Explain how one thing led to the next until this monumental change occurred.

Pump You Up

Activity Sheet

Supporting people is a great way to help them feel better. Many people get a lot of personal satisfaction out of helping others. Remember the saying, "What comes around, goes around". If you support others, the rewards will come back to you ten times stronger.

Imagine that you are playing a team sport, and you are losing. Your star player is just not playing well. The team needs his help to win the game. Your task is to "Pump Up" the player and motivate him to winning.

The team breaks for a time out. They form a huddle to "Pump Up" the player. Fill in the call-outs with the statements that each person will say to the star player.

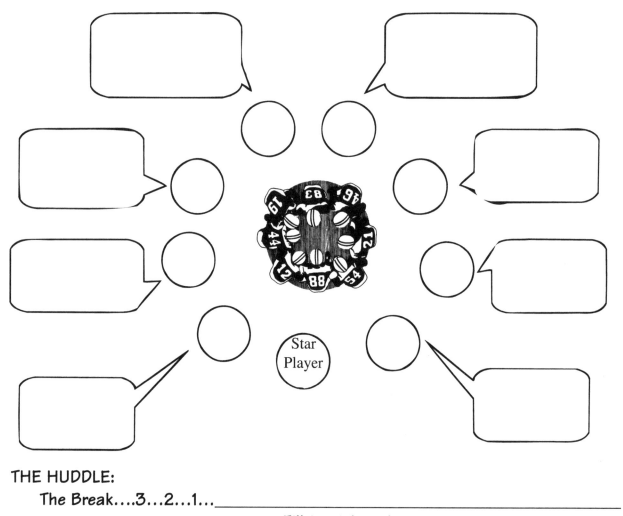

THE HUDDLE:

The Break....3...2...1..._____

Fill-in with a cheer.

Sneakers and Cheaters

Coach Notes

 1. Orientation

Anger is not always obvious. Criticizing, gossiping, giving people the silent treatment, being vengeful, and holding grudges are some of the less obvious ways that anger can be expressed. People who use these kinds of techniques are called "Passive-Aggressive". Usually these people act like nothing is wrong. They deny feeling angry.

Another way some people react is to be a victim. They feel helpless and unable to cope. Victims usually feel sorry for themselves and focus on the negative side of events.

 2. The Challenge
- Describe passive-aggressive.
- List typical passive-aggressive behaviors.
- Learn how to respond assertively to someone who is acting passive-aggressive.

 3. Warm-Up
- Has anyone ever been angry at someone and not told them?
- Why was it difficult to approach the person?
- What would a passive-aggressive person think about anger?
- How would it feel to deal with someone who is passive-aggressive?

 4. Workout
- As a class, decide on a working definition for passive-aggressive behavior.
- Explain that when dealing with passive-aggressive people, it is necessary to stand-up for yourself and ensure that you don't end up being hurt or treated unfairly. One of the most effective strategies is to be assertive and to use an "I message."
- Explain and practice the formula:

  When you…   I feel…   I need…

- Complete the activity sheet individually.

 5. Cool Down
- Ask for volunteers to read their answers out loud. Then discuss the answers together.
- Discuss the benefits to using an "I message."
- Discuss the benefits of trusting your true feelings.

 6. Breakaway
- Ask students to write in their journals about a time they have had to deal with someone who is passive-aggressive.

Sneakers and Cheaters

Workout 14

Activity Sheet

Below is a list of typical passive-aggressive behaviors. Sometimes people engage in these activities without an awareness of how they affect others in a hurtful way. By examining your behaviors and understanding what you do that is passive-aggressive, you can have more control over your thoughts and behaviors and thereby have more positive and productive relations with others. Put a check beside things you have done. Fill in the blank at the end with anything that's not listed.

__ making people feel guilty.

__ forgetting to show up.

__ telling a joke that hurts.

__ being late, and you don't really want to be there.

__ saying something mean, then tell the person you are joking.

__ breaking, losing, or ruining something.

__ talking behind someone's back.

__ putting off doing something.

__ being sarcastic.

__ _____

Write some possible responses to the following two scenarios. Remember to use the "I message" formula.

1. After finally convincing your friend to meet you for a movie, she never shows up after your half hour wait. When you call later, she is not home. You discover that she went out with another friend. The next day she tells you that she just forgot, and you should get over it.

   Your response:_____

   _____

   _____

2. You wear a pair of the latest style of jeans to school. When you see your friend, he sarcastically comments, "Where do you shop, on another planet? "When you look hurt he nudges you and says, "I'm just kidding, don't take it so seriously."

   Your response:

   _____

   _____

You Can't Afford It

Coach Notes

 1. Orientation

When anger isn't managed, it will leave a dent in your life. Problems are difficult to solve, situations get more complicated, and your anger increases. Like other problems, if you don't do something, it gets worse. Many areas of your life become affected: home, work, health, future goals, and aspirations.

 2. The Challenge

- List the consequences of not managing anger in six different areas: school/work, health, friendships/relationships, family, leisure, and future goals.

 3. Warm-Up

- Has anyone ever lost something because they didn't manage their anger?
- Have you noticed other people who have lost something because they didn't manage their anger?
- What are some consequences of losing control frequently?
- If someone's anger became a problem, what would their life be like?
- If someone had a chronic anger-management problem lasting over ten years, what would their life be like? What consequences might result?

4. Workout

- Separate the class into six groups.
- Compile a list of consequences for each of the six categories listed in "The Challenge" above.
- Report the findings to the class.

5. Cool Down

- Ask the students to add additional consequences to their activity sheets.
- Discuss the importance of not "burning bridges" in their life. *"You never know when what you do will come back and hit you."* Sometimes you feel like telling someone off or really giving it back. Stop and think about how this could come back and hurt you. You might think again.

6. Breakaway

- Create a time line to show the progression of the consequences of anger:

Progression Of An Anger Problem

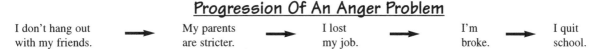

| I don't hang out with my friends. | → | My parents are stricter. | → | I lost my job. | → | I'm broke. | → | I quit school. |

- Write about a time when you felt like losing it with someone but decided to handle it positively and not get angry.

On-Site Reporting

Coach Notes

Workout **16**

 1. Orientation

Violence and aggression has consequences for many people. People are indirectly affected (reading about it in the paper), or they directly experience aggression (being threatened, insulted or physically hurt by another person). In time, violence or aggression affects everyone in one form or another.

2. The Challenge

- Interview ten people of various ages and ask them how violence affected them.

 3. Warm-Up

- What was society like 20 years ago?
- Were people more or less aggressive than they are today?
- How do senior citizens view the level of violence in society today?

 4. Workout

- Have students develop an interview recording sheet in their notebooks.
- Ask students to interview ten people of various ages and record their responses in their notebooks. Have students ask the person they interviewed to sign their name with their responses to ensure that the correct information was transcribed.
- Ask students to answer the following questions in their journals:
    - Out of all of the people you spoke to, what was the most common response?
    - Out of all of the people you spoke to, what answer surprised you the most?
    - If you had to summarize your results into one general statement, what would it be?

5. Cool Down

- Using three poster boards, record the student's answers to the three questions above.
- Have students journal about why they believe things are the way they are today.
- Ask each student to write one thing they are willing to do to help lower the amount of violence and aggression in society. Have them write their response on an index card and display for others to read.

6. Breakaway

- Bring in a speaker, such as a police officer or a social worker, who would have knowledge about the level of aggression in society. Ask them to share their knowledge and expertise regarding violence and aggression.
- Put together a front page of a daily newspaper twenty years into the future. Outline how you would like the world to be in 20 more years. (e.g., no more gangs, children safe on street).

Media Search

Coach Notes

1. Orientation

Most of us are inundated by images of violence and aggression on a daily basis. We see different forms of violence varying in intensity, severity and duration in sports, television shows, videos, and movies. It is estimated that during childhood and adolescence an individual will observe 180,000 violent episodes. Many studies indicate that the effects of viewing violence on television increases aggression and antisocial behavior and decreases pro-social behavior.

2. The Challenge

- Record the violence and aggression on one television show, a movie, a video and a sporting event.
- Determine the result of the violent incident.
- Rate the violent incident on a scale of 1-10.

3. Warm-Up

- What are some current TV shows, movies, videos, or sporting events that appeal to people your age?
- After the list is on the board, ask the student to copy down the list and then put a "v" beside the ones that they would consider having a lot of violence and put a "n" beside the ones that they would con sider non-violent.
- Share the list with a partner and discuss as a class.

4. Workout

- Give each student four copies of the student Activity Sheet to record their observations.
- Do a sample of the Activity Sheet together using a show that the students can recall from memory. This will be for practice purposes.
- Ask the students to fill in the Activity Sheets over the next week. Conduct a review and discussion when the activity is completed.

5. Cool Down

- Have students write a summary about their observations.
- In groups, make lists of non-violent and violent movies, shows, sports, and videos.

6. Breakaway

- As a group write up a list of suggestions for limiting violence in the media.
- Have a debate with one side for allowing violence in the media and the other side against violence in the media.
- Watch a series of cartoons and make a list of the acts of violence, aggression, and discrimination that you observe.
- Create a top 10 list of non-violent movies.

Media Search

Activity Sheet

Over the next week, pay attention to the violence that is portrayed in the media. Use these recording sheets to keep track of your information.

Circle the type of media you observed:

Television Show   Movie   Video (game or music)   Sporting Event

Name of Program _____ Length of Program _____ Date_____

Number of Violent Acts (Keep a tally.)

Total _____

Draw one specific violent incident that you observed.

Explain what happened. _____

_____

Who was the aggressor? _____

Who was the victim? _____

Did they know each other? Yes or No

If yes, how? _____

Why did this incident occur?_____

_____

What was the end result of the violence?_____

_____

If you had to rate this show for the intensity of violence in it, where would it fit on the scale?

mild   1   2   3   4   5   6   7   8   9   10   severe

Angry 8's Half Time Game
Coach Notes

Workout  18

 1. Orientation

Make a copy for each student of the Angry 8's bingo game card. For the teacher's convenience, photocopy the list of questions and cross them off as you read them.

2. The Challenge

- Students will review 62 anger related questions and answers.

3. Warm-Up

- As a review, ask the students to brainstorm a list of terms or concepts that they have studied in the anger workouts.
  Write the list on the board where it can be left for the students to refer to throughout the game, or it can be erased to make the game more difficult.
- Write the list on the board.

 4. Work Out

- The game is similar to bingo. Instead of having bingo cards, each student will have one Angry 8's Activity Sheet.
- Ask each student to circle two rows of squares on their card for a total of 16 squares. Each student will look for their answers within their circled squares. This creates the effect of the students having different cards.
- The teacher will read a question and the students that have the correct answer within their circled squares put a check on the square with the correct answer.
- The first student to check all the squares within their two circled rows calls out "Angry 8's."
- Check the card to verify all the answers are correct. The first student to get all the squares checked in two rows wins.
- Continue playing until there are more "winners."

 5. Cool Down

- Have the students write their own questions and answers to use in another class meeting.
- Give small prizes to the winners.

 6. Breakaway

- Have groups develop a different game to review major information. Use popular game shows on television or develop their own original game.
- Present and play the new games in subsequent lessons.
- Using the same game cards, enlarge the squares and cut out the pieces. Play a matching game (like "Fish") or a memory game (like "Concentration") using the individual squares.

Angry 8's Half Time Game
Questions and Answers

Answers

1. Degrees
2. Tolerant
3. Perspective
4. View
5. Emotions
6. Injustice
7. Frustration
8. Control
9. Insulted

10. Outside
11. Harmful
12. Stand
13. Obstacles
14. Change or solve a problem
15. Hurt
16. Intense
17. Unpleasant

18. Recognize
19. Express
20. Rosa Parks
21. Warning
22. Lance Armstrong
23. Physically
24. Short term
25. Long term
26. Listen
27. Stress
28. Doctor
29. Coping
30. Hard Work
31. Your thinking
32. preventing or provoking

1. There are many different _____ of anger.
2. Someone who is very patient with others is said to be what?
3. What is the word that means "another person's point of view?"
4. The way you _____ an event will have a lot to do with how you respond.
5. Anger is closely related to other _____?
6. When you perceive something is not fair it is referred to as an _____?
7. When you are not able to perform a task, it often leads to _____.
8. When you can not deal with a situation it feels like you are out of _____.
9. If you are put down you feel _____.
10. In many cases how we feel on the inside is different from what we show others on the _____.
11. Anger can be helpful and _____.
12. Anger can make you _____ up for yourself.
13. What do you call small problems that occur in life?
14. What can anger help you do?

15. Anger that is not expressed appropriately will _____ yourself or others?
16. The more _____ and frequent you get angry the worse it is.
17. Being angry is usually uncomfortable and _____.
18. It is important to _____ when you are angry so you can do something about it immediately.
19. It is necessary to _____ your anger in acceptable ways.
20. Who was the person who stood up for herself and refused to give up her bus seat?
21. Anger acts as a _____ that something is wrong.
22. Who overcame cancer and won three consecutive Tour De France cycling events?
23. The body responds _____ to anger?
24. Increased rate breathing rate and heart rate are two _____ effects of anger.
25. Ulcers and heart disease are two _____ effects of anger.
26. Once you know how your body responds to anger, it is important to _____ to it.
27. What is closely related to anger?
28. Who is someone who is specifically trained to deal with stress-related illnesses?
29. Screaming and hitting are examples of negative _____ strategies.
30. Managing anger takes a lot of _____.
31. What greatly influences your anger?
32. People can respond with a _____ response or a _____ response to an incident.

50

Angry 8's Half Time Game
Questions and Answers

33. When something happens to you, it is your _____ what you will do about it.

34. Three ways people express their anger are _____ and
_____.

35. People who do not respect the rights of others are said to be _____.

36. Assertive people stand up for their _____ and respect others.

37. Passive people keep their anger _____.

38. Assertive people express their anger in a _____ manner.

39. Assertive people use a _____ of techniques to express their anger.

40. Assertive people have the best _____.

41. Three ways to respond to anger are: express, escape and _____.

42. Keeping track of anger allows you to notice common _____.

43. Figuring out what makes you angry is to determine the _____ of anger.

44. Finding a solution to your problem is to take _____.

45. The important thing is to _____ from your mistakes.

46. Other than physical, what is the name for signs that the body shows?

47. What do you call the thoughts you say in your mind?

48. What comes between feeling and behavior?

49. What do you call words you say to someone to help, encourage and support them?

50. What do you call the skills necessary to work with others?

51. What do you call someone who keeps anger inside and does sneaky
things to the people they are angry with?

52. What word is used to describe physical force with the intent to harm?

53. It is estimated that children and adolescents will view
more than 180,000 violent _____ on television.

54. What word is used to describe the cost of anger/violence?

55. It is important not to _____ bridges, because it could affect you later in life.

56. Keeping track of your anger, will provide
useful information about what _____ anger.

57. Being _____ is when someone is able
to look at a situation without their personal biases.

58. When it comes to anger, it is important to _____ from your mistakes.

59. Making _____ is the way we learn.

60. When you act _____ you do not think before you act.

61. _____ refers to how often you get angry.

62. A Self _____ is used to determine how you rate yourself.

33. Choice
34. Assertively
and Passively
35. Aggressive
36. Rights
37. Inside
38. Non-threatening
39. Variety
40. Results
41. Explode
42. Problems
43. Cause
44. Action
45. Learn
46. Physiological
47. Self-talk
48. Thinking
49. Support Talk
50. Teamwork Skills
51. Passive-
Aggressive
52. Violence

53. Episodes
54. Consequence
55. Burn

56. Triggers

57. Objective
58. Learn
59. Mistakes
60. Impulsively
61. Frequency
62. Assessment

Angry 8's

Activity Sheet
Game 1

Assessment	Preventing	Assertively	Physically	Change or Solve a Problem	Your Thinking	Long Term ,	Insulted
Express	Degrees	Problems	Lance Armstrong	Impulsively	Stand	Listen	Outside
Rosa Parks	Cause	Tolerant	Explode	Intense	Obstacles	Hard Work	Harmful
Learn	Self-talk	Warning	Perspective	Aggressive	Hurt	Choice	Coping
Control	Thinking	View	Unpleasant	Physio-logical	Short term	Mistakes	Consequence
Frustration	Emotions	Action	Recognize	Violence	Rights	Doctor	Burn
Injustice	Passive-Aggressive	Learn	Objective	Variety	Episodes	Non-Threatening	Triggers
Teamwork Skills	Support Talk	Stress	Passively	Results	Inside	Frequency	Provoking

Be Aware and Beware

Workout **19**

Coach Notes

 1. Orientation

Up to this point you have learned that anger comes in a variety of forms and in many different degrees of severity. You have taken a close look at your own anger/aggression as well as examples of aggression that you witness in society. Now that you are more aware of aggression and you are able to recognize it, it is time to focus on what you can do about it.

Being committed to making some changes in your life requires determination and perseverance. You must remember that it is possible to learn how to respond to anger without using aggression. You can learn some techniques to change your style of thinking for the rest of your life.

2. The Challenge

- List factors that make people more susceptible to getting angry or becoming aggressive.
- List factors that influence your anger.
- List some warning signs that you or someone else is losing control of their anger.

3. Warm-Up

- What factors will influence how quickly a person will get angry?
- Has anyone ever seen someone losing it over what appears to be something quite minor?
- Has anyone ever witnessed someone with an enormous amount of patience and understanding during a completely tense and anger inducing episode?
- What makes people react so differently?
- What are some red flags or warning signs that someone is going to lose control of their anger?

4. Workout

- Read through the information on the Activity Sheet about losing control and discuss.
- Complete the Activity Sheet and discuss answers in small groups.
- Using two charts, list factors that would make someone less patient and more patient when dealing with anger.
- Make a list of personal warning signs that might indicate they are losing control.

5. Cool Down

- Discuss methods of stopping people who are in the tunnel? What is a safe thing to do?
- What are some strategies to use once you start to see the red warning flags? How do you stay out of the tunnel?

6. Breakaway

- Design a picture to represent what it is like to be caught in the tunnel.
- Write in journals about a time they felt like they were caught in a tunnel.

Be Aware and Beware

Activity Sheet

Have you ever been so angry that you felt like you were stuck in a long dark tunnel? A tunnel where you didn't notice what was going on around you, and you didn't hear anything or see anyone? If you get to the point where you can no longer think rationally, you have lost control. Many people who fight say they don't notice what was going on around them. In some cases they don't even remember anything about the fight. It is difficult to stop someone once they have lost control. It is like trying to stop a diver midway through a dive or a luge rider halfway down the run.

Use the space below to write about a time when you lost control. What happened? How did you feel before, during and after? What kind of comparison could you make to describe how you felt? If you need more space, feel free to use the back of this sheet.

_____

_____

Red Flags

Everyone has their own series of red flags or warning signs that they are going to lose it. What are yours?

> Warning signs that you or someone else is about to lose control of their anger.

> Factors that contribute to a person being less patient and less able to control their anger.

When you notice one or some of these signs, it is time to **STOP AND BE AWARE!**
Stop everything you are doing and note how you are feeling. Be aware of your anger.

FIRST AID FOR ANGER STEP 1: _STOP_

Break for Ice Cream

Coach Notes

Workout **20**

 1. Orientation

The second step for anger first aid is to **BREAK** the cycle. This may be done several ways. You can **physically** remove yourself from a situation for one minute, an hour, or even longer. You can go for a walk, exercise, or anything else that works to help you calm down.

You can also **mentally** distance yourself from a situation by doing something else with your mind (e.g., count backwards from ten, take deep controlled breaths, think of a calm place, recite a poem or song in your head, or focus or concentrate on an object or picture). Take a break using any method you want. The key idea here is to break the behavior so that it does not continue in its destructive path.

2. The Challenge

- Learn and use the "ICE CREAM" techniques for control.

3. Warm-Up

- What are some effective ways of dealing with anger?
- What works? What doesn't work when you are trying to get rid of anger?

4. Work Out

- Go through the ICE CREAM steps as a large group. After explaining each step give the students a copy of the Activity Sheet so that they can refer to it during the workout.
- Ask the students to practice using the steps over the next month. Have students make copies of the data collection sheet (a sample is included on the bottom of the student activity sheet) into their notebooks to record their results.
- Have them add additional techniques that they tried as well.

5. Cool Down

- Out of all the techniques, which one will work the best for you and why? Which one do you think will not work for you and explain why? Record thoughts in a journal.
- How could you use the "ICE CREAM" techniques for something other than controlling anger? Record answers on the board.

6. Breakaway

- Put a sample of various music clips together. Have the students record their feelings and mood while listening. Record their answers and then compare with classmates. Discuss that music is individual. Each person will have a unique response to music.
- Have students role-play to demonstrate how to use "I messages" to be assertive.
- Rate how well the "ICE CREAM" technique works each time you use it (1= poor, 5= very well) and chart or graph the results.

Break for Ice Cream

Activity Sheet

Here are some ideas to help you work through angry situations. The following ideas are called anger control techniques. Remember the phrase "Take a Break for Ice Cream" to recall the different techniques. Each letter in the word "ICE CREAM" stands for a different technique to break the cycle of anger.

IMAGINE SOMEWHERE CALM

Thinking about a nice place can have a pleasant effect on your body. The best part about this is it can be anywhere you want.

COUNTING BACKWARDS

Counting backwards from twenty slowly and steadily can help you get control of yourself. It gives you time to STOP... THINK... THEN ACT.

EXERCISE

Not only will exercise help you calm down, but it will also help to prevent anger from occurring. When your body is healthy, your mind is healthy.

CONSEQUENCE ACCEPTANCE

Sometimes we make mistakes and there is a logical consequence that follows. In some cases, accepting the consequences without becoming discouraged is the best reaction.

RELAXATION TECHNIQUES

Learning to relax is a skill that many people could use. Some common techniques are: taking deep breaths, head-to-toe tension and relaxation, or visualization. Athletes often use this technique before an event to help them relax and concentrate.

EITHER SOLVE IT OR LEAVE IT

Sometimes just walking away from a situation is the best thing to do because the time is not right to begin to solve it. Problem solving is a technique to use to find a solution to a problem or to negotiate with another person.

ASSERT YOURSELF

There are several methods to be assertive. One of the most common methods to be assertive is to use an "I message". Here is the formula:
When you _____ I feel_____. I need _____ .

MUSIC

Music can help to change your mood. Lively music makes you feel energetic, slower music might help you calm down. Music can also help to distract some negative feelings and help you put yourself somewhere else that is more positive.

FIRST AID FOR ANGER STEP 2: BREAK

Data Collection Sheet: Copy the following form into your notebook six times.
The technique I used is:_____   When I used it _____
On a scale of 1-5, with 5 being the best, how did it work? _____
What was the result?_____

Think Tank

Coach Notes

 1. Orientation

The third step in first aid for anger is to **THINK**. This is a difficult step because you need to use every bit of energy to control your mind and **think** about the best way to respond.

In addition to thinking positively, you need to think about your best response to the situation. You need to ask yourself if your my response will be helpful or harmful? Use the THINK Step to go through possible responses and their outcome.

2. The Challenge
- Learn how to use the THINK Step to respond to anger.
- List a variety of possible responses to a problem and determine whether they are helpful or harmful.
- Learn the difference between justified anger and unjustified anger.

3. Warm-Up
- What is the difference between a helpful response and a hurtful response to anger?
- What are examples of situations where anger is justified? unjustified?

4. Workout
- Write down a helpful and a hurtful response to each scenario below:
    1. You find out a good friend has been talking behind your back.
    2. Someone steals your bike.
    3. You fail a final exam.
    4. Your pen exploded and ruined your shirt.
- Complete the student Activity Sheet.

5. Cool Down
- Share the responses from the Activity Sheet with a partner. Help each other ensure that the responses fit the categories.
- Journal about a time you responded to an anger or stress inducing event in a helpful way.

6. Breakaway
- Split the class into two teams and have each person on the team write an anger inducing event. Put all of the situations into a hat/basket. Ask one person from each team to come up and pick a situation. They must say a response in 10 seconds. If it is helpful they get one point, if it is harmful they get 0.
- Transfer all of the situations to a board or overhead so that the students can copy down the list. Using the situations from the team game, write a positive statement you could say to yourself for each situation. It should be encouraging, supportive and a positive response to the situation.

Think Tank

Activity Sheet

There are times when anger is justified and there are times when it is unjustified. Sometimes anger is a natural response to a situation. You might have been lied to, cheated on or treated unfairly. There are times in life that people will intentionally and knowingly hurt others. Even "justified anger" has to be responded to in a helpful way. It doesn't give you permission to hurt the other person back. Anger is not wrong, but what you do with it can be wrong. When you recognize that anger is justified, then you need to express it in a helpful way. If you express yourself by punching, swearing or yelling, then anger will surely hurt you in the end.

Write three examples of justified anger and three examples of unjustified anger. For each example list a helpful response and a hurtful response.

Justified Anger	Helpful Response	Hurtful Response
1.		
2.		
3.		

Unjustified Anger	Helpful Response	Hurtful Response
1.		
2.		
3.		

FIRST AID FOR ANGER STEP 3: THINK

No Reaction

Coach Notes

 ### 1. Orientation

The last step in first aid for anger is to **RESPOND**. The key here is to **RESPOND** to anger and not to React to your anger. Reacting is usually impulsive and it leads to a much more serious problem. When you react you tend not to think sensibly about what you are doing nor do you consider the consequences of your behavior. When you respond to anger, you are the one in control and you try your best to solve the problem. Responding involves maintaining control of your behavior and thinking sensibly. It requires you to use patience in responding to your anger.

It is your choice. You can't control what the outcome of a situation will be, but you can do your very best to influence the end result by responding effectively.

2. The Challenge

- Learn how to respond assertively to anger.
- Learn the difference between reacting and responding.
- Use the acronym "PATIENCE" to respond assertively and positively.

3. Warm-Up

- What is the difference between react and respond?
- What are some of the consequences to reacting to anger?
- What is an assertive response? How does an assertive person look and behave?
- How can you respond to anger without hurting someone?

4. Work Out

- Ask a volunteer to show how you should look if you are trying to be assertive.
- Get suggestions from the class to make their stance more meaningful.
- On a blank piece of paper, draw and label the parts of an assertive person (e.g., shoulders square, head up, eye contact.)
- Introduce and explain the PATIENCE Principles.
- Put the acronym on an overhead for 30 seconds and then take it off. Ask each student to see if they can remember what it all stands for. Write it down on a piece of paper.

5. Cool Down

- Write in a journal about whether you usually react or respond to anger.
- Have students write about a person they know who is assertive.

6. Breakaway

- Ask groups to role-play a "what not to do scene" and a "what to do scene" related to being assertive Ask the audience to point out what is right and what is wrong.
- Choose one of the scenarios from the activity sheet and act out the assertive response using the PATIENCE Principles.

No Reaction

Activity Sheet

In order to solve conflicts and manage your anger in a positive and assertive way, it's important to know how to RESPOND in a patient and productive manner.

Being patient with yourself and others will allow you to communicate most effectively. Use the "PATIENCE PRINCIPLES" to help you remember the following practical tips on how to best stand up and express yourself assertively.

P Pick a good time and place to talk.
A Avoid using general words like "never" and "always." E.g., "You always interrupt me."
T Talk about only one issue at a time.
I "I messages" work the best. Eg., "I feel hurt that you forgot to call me."
E Eliminate exaggeration and criticism.
N No put downs or insults.
C Clarify what you mean to say and what you hear the other person say.
E Examine and explore other possible points of view and different opinions.

Remember that if you ever feel like you are losing your patience, take a time out and try talking to the person later. In some circumstances it is best to wait until either you or the other person is calm and willing to solve the problem. This could be an hour, a day or longer. You will gain a lot of respect if you RESPOND with patience and not react to anger.

The following scenarios are situations where both people will need to respond using the "PATIENCE PRINCIPLES" to express their anger and attempt to solve their problem. In your notebooks, write what you would say or do for each situation. Remember to use the PATIENCE PRINCIPLES.

1. You are in the middle of a party and your date starts to hit on one of your best friends. What will you do at the party? What will you say? What will happen later?

2. You come to school with a new haircut and three of your friends burst out laughing and embarrass you in front of the whole class. What do you do? What will you say? When will you say it?

3. You have been waiting in a restaurant for over thirty minutes for a table and you were told when you came in that it would only be about five minutes. What would you do or say?

4. Your boyfriend/girlfriend has interrupted you five times in the last three minutes of you telling him/her what a horrible day you had. What could you say?

FIRST AID FOR ANGER STEP 4: <u>RESPOND</u>

Putting it All Together
Coach Notes

 ### 1. Orientation

Training yourself to become aware of your thoughts and feelings, your attitudes and behaviors will help you control anger. Just like any training program, anger-management training works best if it is done over a long period of time. Making smaller steps towards a goal is better than taking no steps at all. Be patient with yourself and others and you will see tremendous rewards.

Just like an athlete, if you do not maintain your program, you will lose it. If you don't apply what you have learned then it will be lost. Keep practicing, reviewing and applying what you learn. Being able to transfer what you learn to your real life is the single most important aspect of any training program. If you don't use it, you will lose it!

2. The Challenge

• Develop an original comic strip to show how to use the 4 first-aid tips for controlling anger.
STOP — BREAK — THINK — RESPOND

3. Warm-Up

• Why would the four steps be referred to as first-aid?
• What are some examples of situations that you may want to use the first-aid steps?
• In groups, have students examine the comics they created.
• Brainstorm a list of tips and writing tools for developing a comic.

4. Work Out

• Give each student 10-15 sticky notes and ask them to write a comic strip (one frame per note) to illustrate how to use the first-aid steps to avoid violence and aggression.
• Ask each student to share their draft with three people, two students and one adult.
• Put a final draft of the comic onto heavier paper

5. Cool Down

• Ask volunteers to read their comics to the group.
• Put all of the class comics into an anthology to keep in the class.

6. Breakaway

• Put together a puppet show or skit for younger children to teach them the four steps.
• Act out the comic strip in small groups and perform for the class.
• Write a rap or song to teach people the four steps.

Signing the Contract
Coach Notes

 ### 1. Orientation

You have learned all about anger, now it is time to do something about it. It is time to make a contract or a promise to yourself. This is for you and nobody else. You own this one—it's all yours. Decide to think, feel or act a new way. Create a new you. Use what you have learned so far to make a change for the better. Be honest with yourself. Get help from people who you can trust if you need to. If you are able to make a personal pledge and stick to it, you will take a very large step toward gaining more self control and self appreciation.

 ### 2. The Challenge

Each student will write their own personal contract or promise to make a change.

 ### 3. Warm-Up

• What are some examples of behaviors, thoughts or feelings that some people might want to change? (E.g., giving more compliments, accepting criticism, swearing less, being more honest.)
• What are some examples of contracts? (E.g. wills, purchase agreement, salary, sports, etc.)
• What are some of the characteristics of a contract? (E.g. clearly written, simple language, specific targets or amounts.)

 ### 4. Work Out

• Using the contract form on the student Activity Sheet, each student will write a personal contract, to start or stop a particular thought, feeling or behavior.

 ### 5. Cool Down

• Why is it important to set goals?
• What are some examples in life where you might want to write and contract or set personal goals (E.g. lose weight, go to university, get a better job.)
• Who are some people who you could go to if you wanted support achieving your goal?
• It is helpful to give yourself small rewards or incentives to help celebrate your successes no matter how small or large they are. Brainstorm for a list of possible rewards.

 ### 6. Breakaway

• Draw a series of pictures to symbolize the various stages of you achieving your goal.
• Create a "Top Ten" list of how you will be a better person for keeping your contract.
• Write an ending to the statement "By keeping my personal contracts, these three things will be different…" Write this on a business-size card and keep in a wallet for when you need a bit of encouragement. On the back of the card, write three of your personal rewards.

Signing the Contract

Activity Sheet

Contract to Start or Stop a kind of thinking, feeling, or a behavior.

I _____ make the following
(full name)

promise to myself in an effort to better manage and control my anger. I promise to:

_____

_____

If at any time I need help keeping this promise, I will:

_____

_____

The people who will know about this contract are: _____

_____   _____
(name of witness)   (signature of witness)

and

_____   _____
(name of witness)   (signature of witness)

This contract was signed and dated this _____ day of _____, _____
(day of month)   (month)   (year)

in _____ .
(place)

_____
(Your signature)

Say What?

Workout **25**

Coach Notes

1. Orientation

Listening and speaking skills are valuable tools for life. Without these basic skills, people are often misunderstood and misinterpreted. Anger is often the result of a misunderstanding or a lack of information. In many cases, just talking openly about the issue will solve it. If someone looks angry, ask them what is wrong. It might have nothing to do with you at all, or they might be angry about something that could easily be solved. Anger has a habit of snowballing, getting worse by the minute, when it is left on its own.

2. The Challenge

- Learn the "FOLDER" techniques for active listening.
- List positive and negative listening attributes.
- Demonstrate positive listening techniques.

3. Warm-Up

- How can you tell when someone is listening to you?
- Have you ever been speaking to someone and you could tell that he was not listening to a word you were saying? What did he do? What did you do? How did you feel?
- Are there people that you could know that are very good listeners? What do they do? How do you feel while talking to them?

4. Work Out

- Put several objects in a big garbage bag such as a basketball, football, racquet, hockey stick, baseball bat. Have one person in each group pick an object, keeping it a mystery to their group members. The person who knows the object must describe it in detail, without saying what it is or how it is used. The group members draw the object. Discuss what was easy or difficult about the activity.
- Make two columns on the board or on chart paper and label: "Good Listening" and the other "Poor Listening." Brainstorm a list of attributes for each side.
- In groups, develop two short skits: one to demonstrate poor listening and another to demonstrate good listening. Use the activity sheet to record observations.

5. Cool Down

- Discuss what is difficult about being the speaker or the listener.
- What were some of the distractions each person encountered?
- Why are some people better listeners or speakers?

6. Breakaway

- Write about a time that a story got completely mixed up due to poor listening or speaking skills.
- Have each student compile a list of listening/speaking skills that they would like to work on improving in the future.
- Write a top ten list of annoying listening habits.
- Play different musical rhythms with a variety of instruments and have students repeat the rhythm back using an instrument or by written symbols.

Say What

Activity Sheet

FOLDER of Active Listening Tips

To help you remember the Active Listening Tips, remember the word, FOLDER.

F   Face the person who is speaking: It is very important to look at the speaker and to sit opposite him or her when it is possible. If it is not possible, turn your head so that you are facing the person who is speaking.

O   Open body language: Having open body language means that you look like you are eager to hear what the speaker is saying. This means that you do not cross your legs or your arms and that you sit up straight.

L   Lean toward the speaker: Leaning slightly forward toward the speaker is another helpful tip.

D   Do not interrupt: Interrupting stops the speaker and it may cause him or her to forget what he or she was going to say. Wait for a natural pause in the sentence, or wait until the speaker is finished talking.

E   Eye contact: Keep your eyes on the speaker at all times.

R   Respond to the speaker: Tell the speaker what you heard him or her say.

Work in small groups to create, and act out, a skit showing poor listening skills and another showing good listening skills. During each of the skits, use this sheet to record the positive and negative habits used by the listeners. Also make notes about your positive and negative observations of the speaker. Use blank paper to record your findings. In the space below write a summary of what you observed.

_____

_____

_____

_____

_____

_____

Use the back of this sheet to write more of your observations.

Increasing Your Flexibility

Coach Notes

 ### 1. Orientation

How flexible are you? Would you consider yourself stubborn or easy-going? Do you give in or fight to win? Do you argue just for the sake of it or do you try to avoid anger at all costs? Do you always think of what you wished you had said long after the argument? Every story or problem has two sides. Achieving a mutually agreeable solution requires looking at the situation from another person's perspective and being willing to negotiate, compromise and problem-solve.

2. The Challenge

- Define and understand the three terms: Negotiation, Compromise and Problem-Solving.
- Demonstrate proper use of the "That's Fair" strategies for Negotiation and Compromise.

3. Warm-Up

- Has anyone ever been locked into an argument (unable to get anywhere with the other person)?
- Has anyone ever felt stubborn and unwilling to give in just to prove a point?
- Put three interlocking circles on the board. Label the three circles Negotiation, Compromise, and Problem-solving.
- Brainstorm words that fit under each heading. Where the circles intersect, list words that fit them both or all.

 ### 4. Work Out

- Put the following opposites on the board or on a chart and have students write the best word to put in the middle (e.g., black-grey-white)
  -black-white, heavy-light, soft-rough, tough-weak, beginner-expert, athletic-couch potato, freezing -boiling, bottom-top, friend-enemy, cheap-expensive, straight-crooked, excellent-awful.

- Explain that in arguments usually one person takes one side and the other person takes the other side. They push and pull and never seem to solve the problem. The goal of the negotiation is to have an agreement that both sides agree with.
- Pass out an Activity Sheet to each student. Discuss the acronym "That's Fair" Explain that these are helpful tips for compromising, negotiating, and problem-solving. Use them as rules or a for mula to work out a problem.
- Have the students work in pairs to write a typical problem or dilemma that they might encounter. Ask one person from the pair to come up and choose a scenario and write a solution using com promise or negotiation. Present the problem and the solution to the class and ask for feedback/ discussion. Ask each pair to write their solution on the bottom of the Student Activity sheet.

5. Cool Down

- Discuss what was easy or difficult about reaching a solution.
- Journal about a current problem/difficult situation.

6. Breakaway

- Look in a current newspaper and find a story about people/businesses/agencies who are trying to negotiate a compromise or solve a problem. Present the article to the class and discuss.
- Write a cartoon where you use the "That's Fair" Tips to demonstrate how to solve a problem.

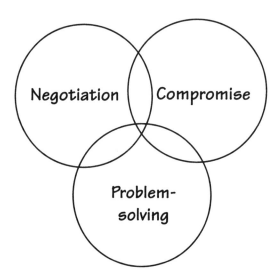

Increasing Flexibility

Activity Sheet

Below are the "That's Fair" strategies that can be used when you are trying to negotiate, compromise, or problem-solve.

T ry to understand what the other person is saying.

H ear how they feel.

A gree with something they said.

T ell your side.

S tate how you feel.

F ind the main issues.

A llow discussion of the issues and look for a solution.

I dentify and agree to a solution.

R eview and evaluate the process.

Our Problem:

_____

_____

_____

_____

Our Solution:

_____

_____

_____

_____

Feel free to use the back of this sheet if you need more space.

Defense Defense

Coach Notes

 1. Orientation

You can not control someone else's behavior or feelings, but you can choose how you will act, think and talk to them. In some instances, you will need to defend yourself from someone who is angry with you. A defensive strategy is a plan for positively responding to an angry person. If the strategy does not work, try something else.

 2. The Challenge

- Demonstrate quick responses to deal with anger.
- Create their own original moves, plays or sport terms to describe other positive methods of dealing with difficult situations.
- Design a poster to illustrate one of the concepts on the student activity sheet.

 3. Warm-Up

- What are some typical responses to anger?
- What are some ways that we can choose to react to someone who is angry?

 4. Work Out

- Give each student the activity sheet and discuss the various situations and responses. In small groups, list other original situations and strategies.
- When all of the information is stated, assign each group one situation/strategy and have them design a poster to illustrate the concept. They may choose to use magazines, newspapers, cartoon drawings, sketching, abstract art, objects from nature or anything that they think would work best.

5. Cool Down

- Have one person from each group, present their poster to the class.
- Discuss the danger of trying to reason with an aggressive person.
- Provide (or develop as a class) a list of emergency contact numbers in the event that students are living in an abusive home, or they are in an abusive relationship. Have this list available at all times and ensure that the help numbers/addresses are displayed throughout the entire unit on anger.
- Ask students to write contact information on the front of an index card and a brief description of the service on the back. Keep cards in a box for students to access.

6. Breakaway

- Role-play the various strategies and have the class guess which one it is.
- Find an example of a defensive strategy used in a movie and bring it to class to share.

Defense Defense

Workout 27

Activity Sheet

Defensive moves

If you do something to set someone off…
The Give and Go: You might just need to accept the fact that you are not perfect and you need to apologize and then let it go.

Someone is physically, emotionally, mentally abusive towards you…
Pass and Run: Just get out of there as fast as you can. Don't even try to reason with him or her. Talk to someone you trust and who can and will help you deal with the situation.

You and someone you know have a disagreement and he or she is legitimately angry with you….
Double Header: This doesn't mean fighting or yelling, it means talking to the person and letting him or her know how you feel and then attempting to work out the problem

You realize midway through an argument that it really isn't worth it…
Curve Ball: Do something unexpected, tell a joke, smile, laugh, don't forget to apologize when you have been out of line.

Someone is angry with you and he is doing nasty things behind your back…
Play Offense: Confront the person, tell him what you think is going on, how you feel about it and what you would like to have happen to solve the problem.

When someone just wont leave you alone or just will not drop the subject….
Defense Defense: Keep doing what you are doing. Tell the truth, be assertive, use active listening, and do everything in your power to help solve the problem.

Your own defense strategy: (Remember it must be a positive method.)

Name of strategy:

_____

When you would use it:

_____

How it would work:

_____

In your group, design a poster to illustrate your defense strategy. Use one from the list given or use the one you developed.

The Water Bottle

Coach Notes

Workout **28**

 1. Orientation

Dealing with anger is part of life. Everyone has to do it at one point or another. You can't escape from it. Dealing with anger is like a series of bumps in a road. Picture a motocross rider. The rider has to take the whoops (bumps) as well as the smooth ride along the berm (the outside wall). The whoops are the challenging yet deserving part of the ride. The ride on the berm is smooth and allows you to build up speed. We all have smooth times and rough times in our lives. The key is to ride the best you can and use what you learn to take on the next set of whoops. Remember to look out for other riders and keep your head up so you can see what is coming your way.

 2. The Challenge

- Learn that keeping anger inside is not generally the best solution.
- List events that have happened that still make you angry.
- Discuss some positive ways to get rid of residual anger.

 3. Warm-Up

- Has anyone ever blown up at something little? Why did this happen?
- What can you do about things that still cause you anger?

 4. Work Out

- Have each student bring a clear small size empty water bottle to class or buy a case of water and give it to the students to drink before beginning the activity.
- On slips of paper, write down situations that have happened in the past that still anger them.
- Stuff the paper slips into the bottle. They can fold (crumple) up the paper or make it visible. The paper can be any size. Some may want to use larger sized paper for bigger issues.
- Stuff the paper slips into the bottle. Discuss how some people may have a stuffed bottle and others will have an emptier bottle. For those with a full bottle discuss what might happen if you keep stuffing it with more paper?
- Culminate with the sutdents working in pairs to complete the Activity Sheet. This will provide an opportunity for the students to identify and practice healthy methods of dealing with their anger as opposed to "stuffing" their anger.

5. Cool Down

- Turn the bottle into a positive message in a bottle by sending a message or affirmation to a friend or family member. Put the message in the bottle and decorate the outside if desired.

6. Breakaway

- The message in a bottle activity could continue with the student giving the bottle to someone special and then changing the message for the person on a weekly or monthly basis. Nicer bottles can be substituted for the plastic water bottle to make it more meaningful.
- Ask the students to fill their bottle with objects to represent their personality. Use paper, garbage, nature, art supplies, etc. Have the students present their bottle to the class and discuss why they chose the objects they did.

The Handshake

Workout **28**

Activity Sheet

Dealing with anger is part of life. You'll never make anger disappear, but the challenge is to learn positive ways of dealing with it in a straight forward fashion. Keeping anger bottled up is as distructive as unmanaged, hurtful anger.

On each of the fingers and thumb on the hand below, list a technique that you can use to manage anger in a productive way. Next "shake hands" with your partner so that between you, there are ten techniques. You may need to brainstorm additional ideas, if some were the same. Once you have ten anger-management techniques, discuss the merits of each with your partner.

Now choose one anger-management technique that you are willing to practice for the next two weeks. Write it in the blank finger.

Getting It Out for Good
Coach Notes

1. Orientation

Using aggressive techniques such as punching a pillow or ripping up a phone book actually lead to more feelings of anger. Choosing a completely different behavior like physical activity or relaxation is much more useful than reinforcing aggressiveness.

2. The Challenge

- List useful techniques for getting anger out.
- Set a plan for doing one technique over the next month.
- List long-term effects of chronic anger.

3. Warm-Up

- What happens to people who keep their anger bottled up for months on end?
- What are some ways that your health may suffer from prolonged anger?
- Brainstorm for a list of techniques to get rid of anger.

4. Work Out

- Complete the student Activity Sheet individually.
- Survey two people outside of the class for Part B of the Activity Sheet.

5. Cool Down

- Give each student an index card and ask them to write down an original idea for dealing positively with anger. They can use pictures, cut outs, words or drawings to make their card eye-catching. Put all of the index cards on one piece of poster paper and display it in the room

6. Breakaway

- Ask a speaker from the medical field to come in to discuss the physical side effects of prolonged anger such as: heart disease, hypertension, ulcers, depression, migraine, or digestion problems.
- Design a motto or logo for dealing with anger (e.g., "Don't drop the ball— Call.") and put the message on a poster.
- At the beginning of each class, have one pair of students teach an anger reducer. Have other students record the ideas in their journal.
- Give each student a blank calendar and have them write a different activity they will do each day to reduce stress or anger.

Getting It Out for Good

Activity Sheet

It is important to deal with anger before it causes you problems in your daily living. Turning anger inward can lead to feelings of helplessness or depression. A build up of anger can make you unhappy, irritable, nervous, confused and tired. People also report that they seem to lose patience and blow up at even the smallest incident. Some people lose their friends, have difficulty getting along with family members, or they get into trouble at work because of their anger.

Studies have also shown that living with long-term anger can lead to heart disease, ulcers, migraine and stomach problems. If your anger is affecting your schoolwork, job, friendships, relationships or family life, it is time to recognize this as a problem and take steps towards feeling better.

Letting go of your anger is a skill that can be learned. Everyone will find their own unique way to release their anger. Take a look at the suggestions and put a check beside the techniques that might work for you.

Write it out   - write in a journal, write a poem, a letter, or a song
Work it out   - jog, walk, swim, bike, hike, roller blade, skate, ski, surf, or sail
Draw it out   - draw a picture of what your anger looks like or how you feel
Design it out   - make a collage or a clay sculpture
Talk it out   - talk to a friend, a trusted adult or a counselor
Sing it out   - sing a long with your favorite band or sing it out in the shower
Dance it out   - listen to music and dance out your frustrations
Relax it out-   - try Tai Chi, meditation, or Yoga
Laugh it out   - watch a comedian, read some jokes, look at the lighter side of life
Read it out   - read a good book or magazine

What are some additional ways that you can get anger out?

_____

_____

Ask two people the following question and record their response below.
Question: "What do you do to help get rid of built up anger?"

_____

_____

Take A Time Out

Workout **30**

Coach Notes

 ### 1. Orientation

Stress and anger go hand-in-hand. Stress can not be avoided; no one can live without experiencing some amount of stress. Stress may be the result of many different events that occur in our lives such as; worrying about a test, sickness in the family, being unhappy about our appearance, moving, or losing a friend. Similar to anger, our mood on a particular day will affect how we deal with stress. When you have continual stress on a daily basis, your ability to cope with the daily events will be difficult. These events, big or small, can lead to anger because you will not be prepared to deal with the situation. The way you think and feel about events will have a lot to do with how stressed you will feel.

2. The Challenge
• Learn how anger and stress go hand-in-hand.
• Learn how to use breathing exercises and visual imagery as a means to work out stress.
• Design a visual imagery scene.

3. Warm-Up
• What kinds of events/things make people feel stress?
• What do stress and anger have in common?
• What does your body do when it feels stress or anger? (tense, breath quick, difficult concentrating, etc.)
• Where is a place that you would consider relaxing, either real or imaginary?
• Does anyone have a relaxing place that others would not find relaxing? (E.g. Rock concert, swimming underwater)

4. Work Out
• Provide clay, colored paper, and a small box for each student and have them design their relaxing place inside the box (a shoe box works well).
• Explain two quick and immedite techniques for handling stress "Controlled Breathing" and "Visual Imagery." Controlled breathing is the process of inhaling steady breaths, letting the abdomen expand, and then slowly exhaling, letting the abdomen lower. It helps to gently rest your hands on your abdomen to ensure that the breaths are deep and controlled. Visual imagery involves visualizing an image in your mind in an effort to calm yourself down. It is best to practice this technique during non-stressful times to make it easier to recall the picture when it is needed.

5. Cool Down

- Make a title for their relaxing place, e.g., "Just Beachin'" or "Paradise Found" and put it on a card to display.
- Make a collage of relaxing places or activities.

6. Breakaway

- Keep a log book of the times that students use either circle breathing or visual imagery. Record how well it worked.
- Go to a Tai Chi or Yoga school and get an introduction to forms of relaxation.
- Ask several community members to come in to speak about services they offer people to help them relax (massage therapy, physiotherapy, hydrotherapy, someone who works in a spa or a wellness center.
- Invent a new way to visualize tensing and relaxing and teach it to the class (e.g., squishing and orange and releasing it).

* For more information and additional student Activity Sheets on stress, refer in the book "Managing Stress" in *The Tough Stuff: High School Series* by Jan Stewart, published by Jalmar Press.

Building A Team

Coach Notes

 1. Orientation

There will be times throughout the anger workouts where you may want to get more information or support. You may want this help for yourself or for a friend. Sometimes it is easier to get help from someone you know like a teacher or a counselor. Other times you may want to talk to a professional who specializes in helping people with a particular issue. Learning where to go for help and support before you need it is important because you may not have the time to search for help when you, or someone you know, is in a crisis.

 2. The Challenge

- Make a list of community resources where help is provided for people in crisis.
- Write a short description of what each agency/group offers to teens.
- Design a pamphlet or brochure to promote getting help when needed.

3. Warm-Up

- What are some issues that have come up during the anger workout sessions?
- What are some current issues that teens are dealing with?
- What are some agencies/support groups that help teens who have problems?

4. Work Out

- Bring in enough phone books for each group to have one personal and one business directory. Bring in lists or pamphlets of community resources that help teens.
- Have each group develop a list of names, addresses, and phone numbers of resources that teens can use if they need professional help (crisis numbers, family services, mental health, teen clinics etc.) Briefly state the service each group provides.
- Give each student a blank piece of paper and have them fold it into thirds to represent a pamphlet. Each group should develop a pamphlet of resources for teens For example, "Where you could go if…"
- Students may want to use a desktop publishing program to design their pamphlets.
- To vary the activity the teacher may want to have each group target a particular problem such as abuse, medical problem, depression, or family relationships.

 5. Cool Down

- Have each group present their pamphlet to the class and display it in the room.

6. Breakaway

- Ask representatives from various agencies to come in to talk to the class.
- Go on a trip to one of the agencies in the community.
- Have the students do a research project on one of the agencies.
- Interview someone who works at one of the agencies.
- Write an advertisement or a jingle to promote an agency that helps teens.

Deciding on A Play

Workout **32**

Coach Notes

 1. Orientation

Problems are a fact of life. Picture yourself making a decision about where to go for the weekend when two different friends have invited you out. How would you make the decision about where to go? How about trying to decide what kind of job you want or what kind of career you will have? Learning how to work out your problems and making decisions are skills you can use for the rest of your life. Players on a team need to agree on a play in order to score points. They think about consequences, they try to visualize what the other team will do and they decide on a course of action that they believe at the time is the best. If it doesn't work, then try another play and hope for the best.

 2. The Challenge

- Learn how to use the "SOLVE" method to work through a problem.
- Create a list of difficult decisions.
- Make a list of teamwork skills.

 3. Warm-Up

- Using the Activity Sheet review, apply the "SOLVE" acronym for solving problems. Pick a typical teen problem to illustrate the steps.

4. Work Out

- Have groups of student illustrate how to use the SOLVE steps to solve a problem.
- Write out the steps on a chart and present the scenario to the class.

5. Cool Down

- What was difficult about working through the "SOLVE" steps? What was easy?
- Why would problem-solving be a part of working out anger?
- Have each student create their own list of difficult decisions they have had to make in their life or that they anticipate making in the future. Record answers in their notebooks.

6. Breakaway

- Have the students design a tower to illustrate/symbolize the decisions they have made or will anticipate making. Bring in building blocks to use as a stimulus for designing a tower.
- Think about a president of a country, or a CEO of a large company, or someone else who encounters a lot of problems in one day. Create a list of problems that this person would encounter. Label it "A Day in the Life Of _____".

Deciding on A Play

Activity Sheet

Use the following "SOLVE steps" for solving a typical teen problem:

S *State the problem:* State what the problem is and try to be as specific as possible.

O *Outline your options:* Decide what you can do about the situation. Brainstorm all of the ideas you can think of to respond to the problem.

L *List the options you like:* Pick the options that you think are the best. Maybe some of your options could be changed or joined together into an even better idea. At this time you do not have to be worried about details.

V *Visualize the outcome:* Go over some of your responses to the problem situation. Think to your self: "What will happen if…?" "How will it affect what you feel, need, and want?" "How would it affect others?" "How would it relate to what you and your family believe?" Once you have thought about the future using your options, pick the best one and decide how you will do it.

E *Evaluate the Results:* The final step is to decide if you made a decision that helped you or not. Ask yourself, "Did things turn out the way I thought?" "Is the solution better than if I had not done anything?" "What are the consequences of this solution?" Remember just like athletes need to practice their sport over and over again, you may need some practice to find the best solution to solve the problem.

Write the Problem that your group has decided to try to solve below:

_____

_____

On a separate sheet of paper, write what you would do in each the of the "SOLVE Steps" to arrive at a solution to your group problem.

Difficult decisions I have made in my life:

_____

_____

_____

_____

Difficult decisions I anticipate making in the future:

_____

_____

_____

_____

Advisory Committee

Coach Notes

Workout **33**

 1. Orientation

Who do you look to for advice? Think about problems you have had in the past. Who did you talk to? If you had to make a difficult decision, who would you discuss it with? Discussing a problem with people you trust is a good way to become aware of the good and bad points about a decision you are considering and it is a good way to look at something from a different perspective.

 2. The Challenge

- List people who can help solve problems.
- Write typical responses each person would give you for your problem.

 3. Warm-Up

- Make a list of people who usually give us advice when we are faced with a difficult decision (friends, family members, coaches, counselors, elders, principals, teachers, neighbors, people from church.)

 4. Work Out

- Think about a current problem you have.
- Imagine that you are going to hold a committee meeting with all of the people that would give you advice on what to do.
- Record the meeting using the Student Activity sheet.

 5. Cool Down

- Discuss with the Class "Who do you find is a great support to you? Who is on your team? What do you admire about them? What are they like? Why are they important to you?"
- Develop a series of "sports" cards based on people that are a support to you. Paste a picture or draw a picture of the person on the front of the card. On the back of the card, write what makes this person special to you.
- Take a look at a real sports card? Use this to help you design your series. Try to put as many people in your series as possible.

 5. Breakaway

- Write a letter to the people who helped you and send it to them.
- Write a classified ad for an advisory team outlining all of the individual qualities you would like to have on your team.
- Make a list of the ways that you can support your team members. E.g., giving them compliments, sharing information about yourself, or taking time to listen to them.

Advisory Committee

Activity Sheet

A committee is a group of people who set out to accomplish a task. Your committee's task is to solve your dilemma or problem.

1. Put yourself as the chairperson of the meeting.
2. In front of you, write the problem on the table.
3. For each person around the table (your committee members) write their names on the chair. You can draw a picture of them if you wish.
4. Use the bubbles to write what each person will tell you. What advice will they give you?

Remember it is your problem and you own it. They might give you advice or suggestions, but it is up to you to make the final decision.

Write what action you will take in the record of minutes at the end of the meeting.

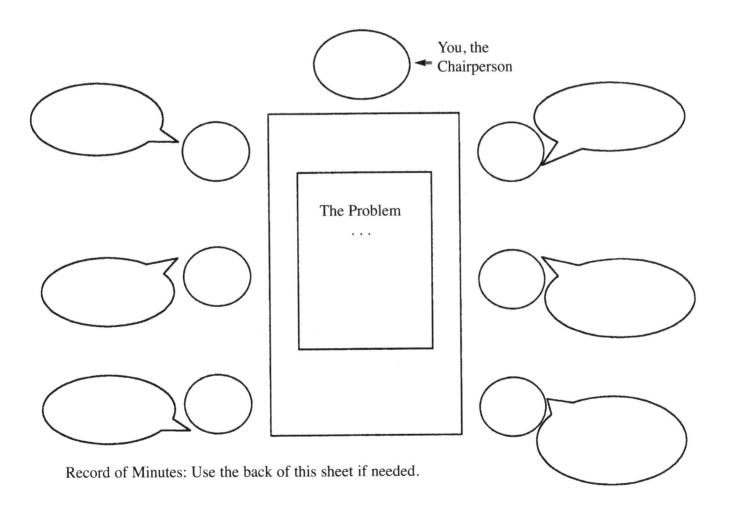

Record of Minutes: Use the back of this sheet if needed.

Four-Wheeling

Coach Notes

Workout  34

 1. Orientation

There are four main areas of our life: spiritual, physical, emotional and mental. In order to live a balanced life, your four areas need to be equalized. Just like the four wheels on an ATV or a car need to be balanced, so do the four areas or "wheels" in your life. Without a balance, you are likely to have a rough and dangerous ride. An ATV with balanced tires makes the ride interesting, challenging, and still very fun. Keeping the four areas of your life balanced also leads to better health, wellness and enjoyment.

 2. The Challenge
- Learn the elements of a balanced life.
- List activities that you currently do to satisfy the four areas of your life.
- List activities that could be added and integrated into your daily living to create a more balanced life.

 3. Warm-Up
- Why is it important to keep a balanced life?
- What could happen if your life was totally unbalanced? How would you think, feel and act?
- Are there certain times of the year when your life is more balanced or unbalanced?
- What would be the benefit of having balance in your life?
- Put four circles up on a board or chart paper with the labels: spiritual, physical, emotional, mental.
- Ask the group to come up with a definition for each category.

 4. Workout
- Have groups of students create a list of activities that could fit into the four areas and then discuss as a class.
- Possible activities:
  Spiritual: connected to friends, belonging to clubs or group, giving to others, volunteering.
  Physical: relaxation, rest, eating properly, looking after yourself (manicure, facials, massages), easy pace of life, movement and activity.
  Emotional: having a life with meaning, setting goals, time alone, reading, learning new skills.
  Mental: challenging activities, learning, having a focus, taking on projects, creativity, art, nature, hobbies, interests, learning a new skill, creating something, inventing something.
- Complete the Activity Sheet individually.

5. Cool Down

- Was anyone surprised at how their tires looked?
- Did anyone have a completely balanced life with four equal tires?
- What are ways that you found to increase or decrease one of the four areas?
- Take some time to reflect on this activity in a journal.

6. Breakaway

- Make a list of one thing you will do for yourself, in the next week, in each of the four areas.
- Tire rotation activity: Trade the four tire diagrams from the activity sheet with another student and have them tell you what areas you need to work on.
- Take part in four activities to help build on the four areas:

  For Spiritual - Go to a senior's home or a hospital to volunteer for an afternoon.

  For Physical - Go to a gym for a few hours and get some activity.

  For Emotional - Watch a comedy or learn how to juggle.

  For Mental - Solve a difficult puzzle, visit an art gallery, or learn how to make something out of recycled materials.

Four-Wheeling

Activity Sheet

Workout **34**

If you imagine that the four tires below represent the four areas of your life: spiritual, physical, emotional, and mental, what do you need to do to have four well-balanced tires? Let air out of some or add air to others? Are they flat? Over-filled? Just right?

How balanced is your life?
On a scale from 1-10, "10 being perfectly balanced" and "1 being unbalanced"? Where do you fit on the scale?

1   2   3   4   5   6   7   8   9   10

In each tire below, write activities that you currently do that help keep your life in balance.

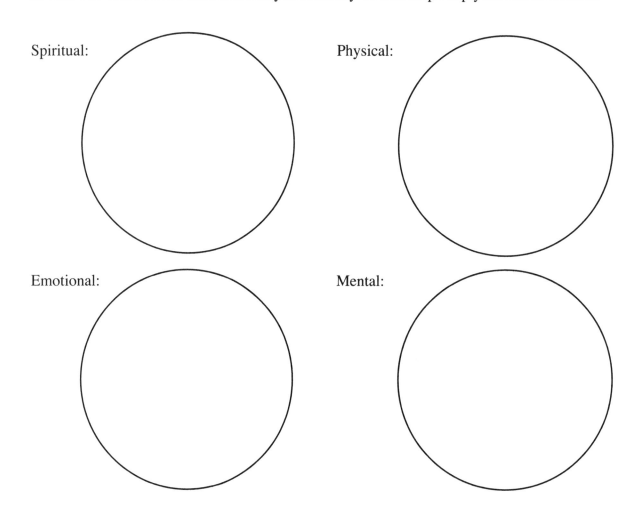

On the back of this sheet write about how you could improve each area of your life? What do you need to do for yourself in order to have more balance in each area?

The Dream Team

Coach Notes

Workout **35**

 1. Orientation

Change is inevitable. Change is constant. Everyone's life has some degree of change. Change is what we need to grow and develop into better people. It can occur in a variety of areas: more knowledge, financial independence, better health, more friends, more fun, and increased happiness, freedom, security or power. In order to change we often dream about what we would really like. Setting a goal is the first step to making a dream become a reality. A goal is a personal target to achieve that leads you closer to a dream. Turning dreams into reality takes courage, strength, perseverance and determination. It is not luck, it is work.

2. The Challenge
- List personal dreams.
- Set goals to achieve personal dreams.
- Use symbols on a dream catcher to illustrate future goals/dreams.

3. Warm-Up
- How do you personally feel about change? How do people you know feel about change?
- Can you think of an example of a time when change seemed negative at the start, but you realized later it was a good?
- What are some changes that we must make in our lifetime?

4. Work Out
- Think back to the Four-Wheeling Work Out where you examined the four major areas of your life. Did you learn anything about what you really value in life?
- Complete the Student Activity sheet.

5. Cool Down
- Who are some people that can help you turn your dreams into a reality?
- Where are some places you could go to get help in achieving your goals?
- What are some obstacles that could make it difficult for you to achieve your goals?

6. Breakaway
- Make real dream catchers and put the symbols in the web. Ask for volunteers to present their dream catchers to the class.
- Use a box in a similar way to the dream catcher, but put the symbols in the box and cover it with a lid. Students can then decorate the outside of the box and keep it as a "hope chest."

The Dream Team

Activity Sheet

What do you want in your life? How do you see yourself in 10 years? in 20 years? What would you be doing if you were successful? What would really make you happy? Think about what you value in life: money, happiness, power, fun, freedom, education.... Write your dreams in the space below.

I dream about…

_____

_____

_____

Now make the first step toward change and turn one of your dreams into a realistic goal. I will…

_____

_____

_____

What do you need to do to help you achieve this goal and turn your dream into reality? The steps I need to take are:

_____

_____

_____

A dream catcher is a traditional symbol that many people believe in to this day. A dream catcher is a decorated net or web of sinew in a circular form that is hung above a person's bed. The net is said to entangle the bad dreams but allow the good dreams to get through and slide down the feathers to the sleeper.

A dream catcher is a personal representation of what is important in your life. It should represent your dreams, wishes, values and goals. Put symbols into the web to illustrate what is important in your life.

DREAM CATCHER

89

Training Schedule

Coach Notes

Workout **36**

 1. Orientation

Now that you have all of the information you need, it is time to get into action. Over the next two weeks, make a concrete plan outlining what you will do to better deal with anger. Start small, don't try to tackle the problem by taking on the hardest thing first. Reward yourself and then move on to another challenge. Celebrate the small successes and allow yourself enough time to get it right.

 2. The Challenge

- Write one goal using the MATCH criteria.
- List ways that you will reward yourself when you are successful.

 3. Warm-Up

- What are the benefits to setting goals?
- Discuss possible goals that students might work on related to anger-management?
- What can you do if your goal is too easy or too difficult?
- What are examples of ways that you could reward yourself if you achieve your goals?

 4. Work Out

- Draw a ladder on the board and show how to make gradual steps toward a big change. For example the bottom rung could be stop swearing at home, then stop swearing at school, then stop putting down friends, then the last one could be to be respectful to partner. Explain that they should set goals that are smaller and in sizeable chunks so that there is a higher rate of success.
- Use the analogy of a high jumper to show the goal increasing slightly so it is manageable.
- Introduce the MATCH criteria for setting goals. (See Activity Sheet.)

 5. Cool Down

- Ask volunteers to share their goals with the class or ask the students to share with a partner.
- Have students draw a pyramid or tower to illustrate anger-management goals they would like to work on in the future, starting from the bottom (easiest) to the top (most difficult).

 6. Breakaway

- Ask an athlete to come to the class to talk about how he or she set goals to achieve their personal best. Have them also discuss how to handle defeat. What are some key ways to move forward after making a mistake or not performing the way you wanted.
- Ask a sports psychologist to come in to talk about some of the exercises athletes do to help set goals, gain confidence, and overcome obstacles.

Training Schedule

Activity Sheet

To help you set individual or group goals, use the following MATCH criteria to guide you.

M <u>M</u>easureable - the goal should be something that can be measured

A <u>A</u>chieveable - a goal should be realistic and the individual or group should be able to achieve the desired outcome.

T <u>T</u>ime Frame - state how long it will take to achieve the goal.

C <u>C</u>lear - a goal should be clear and concise to everyone involved in the process.

H <u>H</u>elp and Support - after you have written your goal, identify people, places, or things that will help you achieve your goals.

Example: My goal is to pass my driving test by Feb. 19th.
In order to achieve my goal, I'll ask my Dad to give me driving lessons on Saturday mornings and I'll read my Driver's Handbook cover-to-cover.

Below write one goal using the MATCH criteria.

_____

_____

_____

_____

_____

_____

_____

_____

_____

_____

When you achieve your goal, what reward will you give yourself for working so hard?

_____

Endurance Run with Hurdles

Workout **37**

Coach Notes

 ### 1. Orientation

An endurance run is a test to see how well you can perform. Hurdles are blocks or obstacles that you must jump over. This game is used to review Workouts 19-36

2. The Challenge

- Review information covered in the second half of the workouts.
- Play a team game called "Endurance Run with Hurdles".
- Reinforce teamwork and cooperation skills.

3. Warm-Up

- Look back over your Activity Sheets at Workouts 19 to 36. What were some of the key concepts we discussed?
- What were some general words or phrases that were used?

4. Work Out

- Split the class into two even teams, and ask them to choose a name for their team.
- On a chart or board, list the team names and under each draw an oval as shown below. The oval represents the track that each team will travel around. The first team to get thirty hurdles will win. This number can be increased or decreased depending on time. As the scorekeeper record the hurdles, she should mark when each team gets a block of ten to make it easier to track.

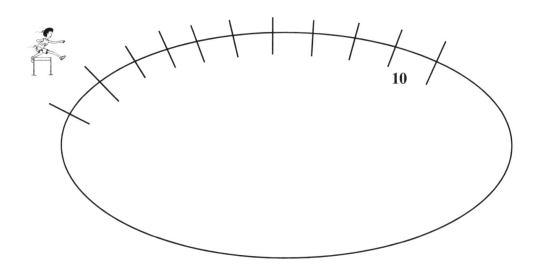

- Alternate asking each team a question from the master list of questions. They may consult other team members to get the answer. For each correct answer the team will get a hurdle(s) marked in their oval.
- The total number of possible hurdle point is indicated before the question, however the teacher will need to make a decision how many hurdles to award a partial answer.
- The questions can also be generated by the students or the teacher may want to write their own. If the students write the questions, put all of them into a box and read them out randomly.
- Some questions are worth more than one hurdle, so read only even questions to one team and only odd numbers to the other so that they have equal opportunity to score.
- If the team is unable to answer the question, the other team can have the opportunity to get the hurdles.
- Toward the end have a sprint around. Have each team stand in a line facing each other. One team will go at a time. Read the remaining questions as quickly as possible and have only one team member answer at a time. The goal is to answer as many questions as possible in the time limit (two minutes). Work through the line up once and see how many hurdles they get.

 ## 5. Cool Down

- Give each team a copy of the questions that they did not get correct and have them find the correct answers.

 ## 6. Breakaway

- Ask each group to make up twenty questions that could be used in a similar game. These questions can then be used in the following Super Bowl Workout.

Endurance Run With Hurdles

Workout  37

Questions and Answers

The number in brackets represents the number of hurdles each question is worth.

1. (2)   What could happen if anger is not dealt with? A: Escalate to violence or aggression.
2. (2)   Anger comes in a _____ of forms and in many different _____ of severity. A: variety, degrees.
3. (3)   List three factors that make people more susceptible to getting angry or becoming aggressive. A: tired, hungry, sick, under stress.
4. (3)   What factors influence our rate of anger? A: Our knowledge of anger reduction techniques, how we were taught to handle anger, current physical and emotional state.
5. (3)   Describe what it is like when people have lost control. A: cannot hear others, cannot think straight, feel like they have tunnel vision, don't know what is going on around them.
6. (1)   What is the first step to controlling anger? A: Stop
7. (1)   What is the second step to controlling anger? A: Break
8. (2)   What is the third and fourth step to controlling anger? A: think, respond.
9. (5)   Describe what it means to break the cycle. A: Physically remove yourself from the situation, walk, exercise or do something to help you calm down.
10. (8) (two per correct answer)What are four techniques that might help someone distance them selves from a situation? A: Count backwards from 10, controlled breathing, think of calm place, recite a poem or song, focus or concentrate on an object or picture.
11. (2) What do "I" and "C" and "E" stand for in ICE CREAM? A: imagine somewhere calm, count backwards, exercise.
12. (5) What does the word "CREAM" stand for in the ICE CREAM strategy? A: consequence acceptance, relaxation techniques, either solve it or leave it, assert yourself, music.
13. (1) What usually happens when we make a mistake? A: There is a consequence.
14. (1) When would you not want to try to solve a problem? A: Other person is unwilling or not ready.
15. (3) What is the formula for making an "I Message"? A: When you….I feel….I need…
16. (2) Explain how music can help you get rid of anger? A: Help you calm down, distract, or feel more positive.
17. (3) How can positive self-talk help? A: encourage, prepare for confrontation, calm down.
18. (3) List three examples of "just" anger. A: being lied to , someone cheating on you, someone steals from you.
19. (3) List three examples of "unjust" anger. A: someone being uncontrollably late, change of plans, someone accidentally bumps you.
20. (3) List three helpful responses to anger. A: talk, express, relaxation, breathing exercises
21. (3) List three hurtful responses to anger. A: put down, yell, throw things, etc.
22. (1) It is important to _____ to anger not to react. A: respond

23. (2) What is the difference between reacting and responding to anger? A: Reacting is defensive and impulsive. Responding is when you are in control and you try to solve the problem.

24. (2) What are two consequences to reacting to anger? A: Say the wrong thing, regret, lose temper.

25. (2) What is an assertive response? A: Standing up for yourself and respecting the other person's rights at the same time.

26. (4, 2 per correct answer) In the PATIENCE Principles, What do P and A stand for?
    A: Pick a good time and place to talk. Avoid using words like never and always.

27. (4, 2 per correct answer) In the PATIENCE Principles, What do T and I stand for?
    A: Talk about one issue at a time. Use "I messages".

28. (4, 2 per correct answer) In the PATIENCE Principles, What do E and N stand for?
    A: Eliminate exaggeration and criticism, No put downs or insults.

29. (4, 2 per correct answer) In the PATIENCE Principles, What do C and E stand for? Clarify what you mean to say and what you hear the other person say. Examine and explore other possible points of view.

30. (1) What will you gain if you respond and not react to anger? A: Respect

31. (1) When is it a good time to try to solve a problem with someone? A: When you are both calm.

32. (4) What are the four first aid tips for dealing with anger? Stop, Break, Think, Respond.

33. (2) What are two ways to make a personal promise to yourself? A: Contract, Set goals.

34. (2 each, total 4) What are two valuable tools for life? A: Listening and Speaking.

35. (6) What does FOLDER stand for? Face the person, Open body language, Lean toward Speaker, Do not interrupt, Eye Contact, Respond to Speaker.

36. (6) What are three ways to become more flexible and define each term.
    A: Negotiation, Compromise, Problem-solve.

37. (5) What does THAT'S stand for in THAT'S FAIR tips for negotiation? A: Try to understand what the other person is saying, Hear how they feel, Agree with something they said, Tell your side, State how you feel.

38. (4) What does FAIR stand for in THAT'S FAIR tips for negotiation? A: Find the main issues. Allow discussion of issues and look for solution. Identify and agree to solutions. Review and evaluate the process.

39. (6) Name three defensive moves and describe how to use them. (Refer to Workout 29.)

40. (6) Name three defensive moves and describe how to use them. (Refer to Workout 29.)

41. (2) What will eventually happen to people who do not deal with their anger? A: blow up, lose temper.

42. (3) List three ways to get rid of residual anger? A: run, walk, hike, read, relax, etc.

43. (2) Anger that has been stuffed away will usually surface with more _____.
    A: intensity.

44. (5) List five techniques for getting rid of anger. (Answers will vary but ensure that they are all positive ways.)

45. (5) List five techniques for getting rid of anger. (Answers will vary but ensure that they are all positive ways.)

46. (1) What often goes hand in hand with anger? A: stress

47. (6, 2 per correct answer) What are three signs/symptoms of stress? A: irritable, often sick, stomachache, headache, confusion, memory loss.

48. (6, 2 per correct answer) What are some common events that often cause stress. A: tests, big assignments, losing someone, moving.

49. (1) What is a de-stressing techniques? A: controlled breathing or visual imagery.

50. (1) What is the other de-stressing technique? A: controlled breathing or visual imagery.

51. (1) For controlled breathing it is important to breathe from your _____. A: abdomen

52. (1) What is a name for people who can help you get through a problem? A: Support Team

53. (2) List two places in the community who can help teens. (Answers will vary.)

54. (2) List two people in the community who can help teens. (Answers will vary.)

55. (2) Talking to someone else about a problem will help you do what? A: See it from another perspective.

56. (4) Who are four people who could help out with a difficult decision? A: clergy, teacher, counselor, parent, friends, coaches, neighbors.

Super Bowl

Coach Notes

 1. Orientation

The Super Bowl Workout represents the final challenge. This workout tests your knowledge of the entire set of 37 workouts.

2. The Challenge

- Review information taught in all of the 37 workouts.
- Play a team game of Dice Football.
- Reinforce team-building skills.

3. Warm-Up

- Spend a few minutes looking through your personal journals and your workout notes.
- Have students journal about what they have learned throughout the anger workouts.
- What surprised you? What did you like and dislike? What did you learn about yourself or others?
- If there was only one thing that you could tell someone to help control their anger, what would that be?

4. Work Out

- Play a game of Anger Football.
- Separate the students into two teams and have them choose a name for their football team.
- Use the questions from Angry 8's Workout, the Endurance Run Workout or from the random list included on the Teacher Question and Answer Page.
- Ask both teams to sit in two rows facing each other. Give each team a copy of the football score card on the student activity sheet. Have them choose a score keeper from their team. Make a copy of the football score card and put it on an overhead projector so that the teacher can keep score of both teams. Mark each play (correct answer on the overhead using a different color of marker for each team.)
- One player from each team will roll a dice. This number (1-6) will indicate how many yards the team will advance down the field. The number on the dice will be multiplied by ten. The teacher will ask the question to one student only. If this student does not know the correct answer, they will be allowed one pass to another player next down the line and they will have the opportunity to answer the question. If they answer the question correctly they will advance that many yards.
- When either team reaches the end zone (getting 100 yards down) they will receive six points. They will then have the opportunity to kick a convert (hard question from the convert question list) for one more point.
- Play for a pre-determined amount of time and see which team can get the most points.

5. Cool Down

- Ask the teams to get together and answer the questions that they did not get correct during the game.
- Ask each team member to shake the other team members' hands.

6. Breakaway

- Ask each team to write questions for another game. Put all of the questions in a box and read them randomly.
- Ask each team to make up their own game to review the anger workouts.
- Ask each person in the class to write one question that they would put on an anger test. Put the questions together and have the class do the test.

Teacher Question Page

The teacher may want to use the left over questions from Angry 8's Half Time Game or from the Endurance Run, or they may use the same questions so that the game is a review of all the workouts. Another option is to have the students write their own questions on an index card and then put all of the questions into a box to be used for the football game.

One Point Convert Questions (following touchdown of 6 points):

1. When tracking your anger, what three things should you pay attention to?
   A: thoughts, feelings and behaviors
2. What is an example of an anger-reducing strategy? A: relaxation techniques, assertion techniques.
3. List three behaviors that usually set people off. A: name-calling, put downs, unfair judgements, pointing fingers, insulting, yelling.
4. True or False. The anger violence cycle often ends on its own. A: False, the Anger violence cycle gets worse with time, unless something is done about it.
5. What are three cues that would tell someone they are getting angry? A: tense muscles, red face, sweating, difficulty concentrating.
6. What are the three degrees of anger? A: Mildly agitated, Annoyed, Enraged
7. What does FITT stand for? A: Frequency, Intensity, Time, Type
8. What is one example of anger blocking self-talk? A: You can do it. Relax. I will do this. Calm down, etc.
9. List three kinds of passive-aggressive behaviors. A: Talking behind someone's back, ruining some thing that belongs to the person they are angry with, being vengeful, silent treatment, holding grudges.
10. What is the I Message Formula? A: When you…I feel…I need…
11. What is an example of reactive aggression? A: throwing, hitting, hurt themselves
12. Define Violence. A: Using physical force with the intent to harm someone or something.
13. What are three consequences to losing your temper? A: reputation as fighter, lose friends, people will be scared of you, legal problems, being banned from places.
14. What are three areas of your life that are often affected by a serious anger problem?
    A: school/work, health, friendships/relationships, family, leisure, future goals.
15. What is one suggestion for limiting violence in the media? A: refuse to watch violence, write letters to stations.
16. True or False. Drugs and Alcohol cause violent behavior. A: False, but they do impair judgement, lower inhibitions and limit self-control.
17. True or False. It is important to react to anger as soon as possible. A: False, you need to respond not react to anger.

18. True or False. Signing a contract is an effective way to make a promise to yourself. A: True
19. True or False. Compromising and Negotiating are helpful methods to solving problems. A: True
20. What does SOLVE stand for? A: State the problem, Outline options, List the good and bad, Visualize the outcome, Evaluate.

Super Bowl

Activity Sheet

Anger Score Card

End Zone	
	0
	10
	20
	30
	40
	50
	60
	70
	80
	90
	100

End Zone

Jan Stewart

B.Ed., P.B.C.E., M.Ed.

Author Jan Stewart has over fifteen years of teaching and counseling experience with students at all levels from Kindergarten to Grade 12. She has taught and counseled at-risk inner-city youth, students from remote northern communities, and adolescents with severe emotional and behavioral disorders. In addition, Jan spent a year teaching and counseling on the Caribbean Island of St.Lucia.

Jan currently works as a high school Guidance Counselor in The River East School Division in Winnipeg, Manitoba. She is a Sessional Instructor for Graduate Studies in Counseling at The University of Manitoba, Department of Educational Administration Foundations and Psychology, as well as a Sessional Instructor for The Faculty of Education at The University of Winnipeg. Jan is also currently writing Health and Physical Education curriculum for the Government of Manitoba.

Previous works include *The Tough Stuff Series: Immediate Guidance For Troubled Students*, published by Jalmar Press, Torrance, California, and *The STARS Program Series*, published by The University of Toronto Press/Guidance Centre in Toronto, Canada, and Hunter House Publishers in Alameda, California.

Jan has conducted numerous national and international professional development seminars for teachers, counselors, administrators, and parents. Jan specializes in the development of creative and interactive counseling tools that are easily implemented into any classroom or counseling program. Jan uses a multi-dimensional approach to learning where her students are active and responsible learners. With fun activities, practical lessons, and realistic strategies, her books offer a very dynamic and unique approach to helping students.

Jan lives in Winnipeg with her husband, Ross, and her son, Jack.